# BUILDING VBA APPS

## Using Microsoft Access 2010

F. Mark Schiavone, Ph.D.

Sycamore Technical Press
www.sycamoretechnicalpress.com

# Preface

Microsoft Access is a powerful database management system. It provides easy to work with tools to assist you in the management of your database.

If you develop applications using Microsoft Access you're already familiar with the creation and management of the forms and reports your end users work with. Although these interface objects offer useful functionality to support your end user's needs, there is a universe of actions missing without including Visual Basic for Applications (VBA) code.

VBA is an easy to learn programming language that underlies every member of the Microsoft Office suite of productivity tools—Word, Excel, PowerPoint, Outlook, and Access all are programmable using VBA. In Access, VBA code can be placed behind any form or report, or can be located in code modules. By including VBA code in your projects the functionality that you create is nearly limitless. VBA is an object-oriented programming language and offers such programming techniques as the creation of your own objects to simplify your code, connecting to external data sources (including Microsoft SQL Server, IBM DB2, Oracle, and MySQL databases), and using COM (component object model) to draw in functionality from other applications such as Microsoft Excel. In short, there is almost nothing you cannot do in Access with VBA code!

This book begins with an overview of the VBA coding environment and then with a primer of the VBA language. We will tour topics that include event models, program flow, sub and function procedures, working with objects (including creating your own objects), code behind forms and reports, and working with user interface elements. Once grounded in these topics, we continue with more advanced subjects such as working with error handlers, using data access objects such as DAO and ADO, and using COM to automate other applications from within Access.

The book is peppered with fully working code examples that are almost always less than a page in length. Each of the major code examples is also to be found in a database file available for download from Sycamore Technical Press and associated with this book title. For more information, visit us at www.sycamoretechnicalpress.com.

## Manual Conventions

Throughout this manual reference is made to various components of the software. Tabs, groups, command buttons, and windows and views appear in boldface type, for example, **OK** and **Font**. Keystrokes appear in boldface italic type, for example, ***Ctrl + V*** and ***Enter***. When possible, the words *select* and *choose* have been used in this manual to allow you the option of using either the mouse or keyboard. Throughout this manual you'll find the following helpful items:

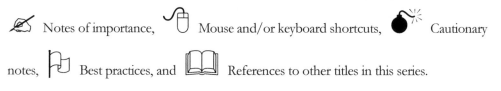 Notes of importance, Mouse and/or keyboard shortcuts, Cautionary notes, Best practices, and References to other titles in this series.

*Italicized* text is used in this book for several purposes. Frequently the first time a technical term is used and appears in the Glossary, it will appear italicized. Italic text is also used when naming database tables, fields, or other objects as well as to enforce emphasis.

# Table of Contents

# Chapter 1 | Introduction to Access VBA

Visual Basic for Applications (for the remainder of this book we will simply refer to it as *VBA*) has been the *de facto* programming language for all members of the Microsoft Office Suite going back nearly to its inception. As its name suggests, VBA is based on the Visual Basic programming language, which itself is based on earlier versions of BASIC. As we'll see, it is a fairly easy language to acquire yet, despite its ease of learning, the language offers some basic components of modern *Object Oriented* programming languages which makes VBA quite powerful as well.

Before we embark on this journey through Visual Basic for Applications the first question should be *why write program code for an Access database?* Since Access 2010 the macro editor has been improved, and many more macro actions have been added to the action catalog, so why bother learning how to write VBA code? Can't macros do everything you can do with VBA? The quick answer: *No.*

These are just a few of the differences between macros and VBA in Microsoft Access 2010:

- Although the **Action Catalog** in the **Macro Editor** has been expanded to include many more actions, it is still a limited set. Because VBA is a *programming language*, you have a nearly unlimited universe of actions you can commit to programming code.

- Macros are limited to a single simple family of program control elements, the **IF..THEN..END IF** (with a few variations involving **ELSEIF** and **ELSE**). VBA has a much richer suite of program control keywords that support branching (as with **IF..THEN..END IF**), jumps, and loops.

- Macros can't solicit input from the end user. They can present a message box with an **OK** button, but not the more complex message and input boxes that VBA supports.

- Macros lack access to the Microsoft Access Object Model, as well as the myriad of Component Object Models (COM for short) that VBA can access. For example, using VBA running behind an Access form, you can create an instance of a Microsoft Word document and populate it with data from the database.

- Macros can respond to errors generated while running, but only in a primitive way. VBA supports a far richer approach to handing errors (as we'll see in Chapter 9).

- You can't pass *arguments* to macros, meaning that most macros must be created to perform a very specific task. A defining feature of a programming language is the ability to create and pass variables (or objects!) to *procedures*. This makes writing flexible and reusable code a reality and is a strong reason why many developers learn VBA.

This list could go on for many additional items but hopefully you see the point. Macros certainly have their place in an application but VBA code offers a nearly inexhaustible source of actions and complex behaviors to bring your Access database into the realm of professionally designed applications.

To provide some grounding in what we'll be discussing, let's take a look at two simple code examples. Following that, the remainder of this Chapter will tour you through the **VBA Editor** interface. We'll begin our formal introduction into the VBA language beginning in Chapter 2.

# A Simple Code Example

Before we continue it might be helpful to review a simple code example. This example should explain why one would want to write VBA code, where VBA code is located, and how it is elicited. For the moment, try not to get too caught up in the details as each of the topics we will briefly explore are more fully discussed elsewhere in the book.

### Closing a Form: *Are you sure you want to do this?*

As mentioned above, macros cannot elicit a response from the end user. This code example does just that. The code is attached to a **Command Button** on a form, as illustrated below.

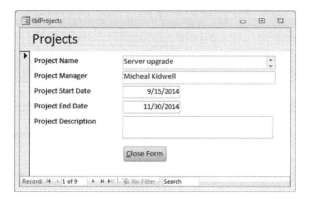

When a user clicks on the **Close Form** button they see the following message box:

The code itself is associated with the command button and is attached to an *event procedure* named *click*, which (as you'd imagine) fires each time the user clicks on the command button. For the code to work we must follow a logical path similar to the following:

Step 1.    Create a *variable* (really a slot in memory) to store the user's response once prompted with *Are you sure you wish to close this form?*

Step 2.    Present a **Message Box** that asks the user this question and offers two choices, *Yes* or *No*. Once the user has selected one of the options (and they must, **Message Boxes** are *modal* meaning you must address them before doing anything else) that choice gets stored in the variable created in Step 1.

Step 3.    Inspect the user's reply and use a simple program flow block to either close the form or keep it open.

The code, located behind a command button named **cmdCloseForm** and attached to the **Click** event, appears as follows:

```
(1)  Private Sub cmdCloseForm_Click()

(2)  'Create a variable to store the response
(3)  Dim intReply As Integer

(4)  'Ask the user if they are sure - store the reply in
        intReply
(5)  intReply = MsgBox("Are you sure to wish to close the
        form?", vbQuestion + vbYesNo, "Close Form")

(6)  'Decide what to do given the reply
(7)  If intReply = vbNo Then
(8)     Exit Sub
(9)  Else
(10)    DoCmd.Close acForm, Me.Name
(11) End If

(12) End Sub
```

The line numbers above do not appear in the actual code—they've been added so we can discuss the code line-by-line. The following table addresses the various parts of this code example.

| Line | Comment |
|------|---------|
| 1 | Declares a *sub procedure* named *Click*. This is actually an *event handler* that is automatically created whenever you place a **Command Button** on a form (many other objects have a *Click* event as well). When the user clicks on the command button named **cmdCloseForm**, VBA knows to go to this point and begin execution of any code. |
| 2 | A comment. Comments are not part of the code execution and in VBA always begin with an asterisk ( ' ). Comments are very useful for assisting a future programmer (which may be you!) document the code's purpose. |
| 3 | **DIM** is a *keyword* that tells VBA to create memory storage space for a variable, here named *intReply*. The *data type* is *Integer*—meaning that the memory storage will be set up to store simple, whole numbers. Working with variables is addressed in Chapter 2. |
| 4 | Another comment |
| 5 | This is where the code prompts the user with the message *Are you sure you wish to close the form?* The **MsgBox** (the keyword that creates message box) statement contains an *argument list*, here contained within parenthesis. There are three arguments present and they are separated by commas (the term is *comma-separated arguments*). The first argument is the *prompt*. The second argument specifies a display icon, as well as sets the kind of reply buttons present (**Yes** and **No**). The third argument sets a title for the message box (see the previous illustration for an example). |
| 6 | Another comment. |
| 7 | This line begins an **IF..THEN..ELSE..END IF** block. If this first test resolves to true (the user clicked the *No* button which causes the message box to store a *built in constant*, **vbNo** in the variable *intReply*) then the next line of code is also executed. Otherwise, the VBA editor jumps past line 9, searching for either another **IF, ELSE,** or **END IF** statement. |
| 8 | This line executes only if the expression on line 7 is true. If so, the **EXIT SUB** statement forces VBA to leave the procedure, basically bypassing any code to close the form. |
| 9 | A default state for the initial **IF** test on line 7. If line 7 doesn't resolve to *true*, this **ELSE** statement will process any other execution. In this case, because the user was only offered two buttons, if they didn't select **NO**, this section of code will execute. We will explore other variations of this and other decision structures in Chapter 4. |
| 10 | This line closes the form using the **DoCmd** object. This object contains many very useful methods, **Close** being one of them. Again we see an *argument list*. Here the first argument is the type of thing to close. The second argument is the name of the thing to close. We're using a shorthand for the name. **Me** refers to the parent hosting the currently-running code. **Name** is a property of me that returns the formal name of the object (in this case the form we wish to close). Objects will be explored in Chapter 6. |
| 11 | Denotes the end of the **IF..THEN** logic block. A way to denote the end of a program control block is mandatory in programming languages. |
| 12 | The end of the **Click** sub procedure for the **cmdCloseForm** command button. If program execution gets to this point it automatically stops. |

## Changing or Deleting a Field Value: Are you sure?

In the previous code example, the code was initiated when the user clicked on a **Command Button**. In this example the code will be triggered by a slightly different path—a data event.

As you know, Access will prompt you if you attempt to delete an entire record, but not if you attempt to delete or change a particular field value. That action requires VBA code.

The trigger for this code example is the **BeforeUpdate** event. Common to many bound objects such as forms, reports, and text boxes, this event fires when there is an attempt to change data but before the change is actually committed to the table (that event is called **AfterUpdate**—events are discussed in Chapter 3). The code will begin by determining whether the user is *deleting* the field value or *changing* the field value. We can probe this by testing the *value* property of the text box. If empty, the user deleted the contents, otherwise the edit is an attempt to change the contents.

As in the previous example, the line numbers are added here for reference only.

```
(1)  Private Sub ProjectName_BeforeUpdate(Cancel As Integer)

(2)  Dim intReply As Integer

(3)   If Me.ProjectName.Value = "" Then
(4)     intReply = MsgBox("Delete Project Name?", vbQuestion +
        vbOKCancel, "Delete Project Name")
(5)   Else
(6)     intReply = MsgBox("Change Project Name?", vbQuestion +
        vbOKCancel, "Change Project Name")
(7)   End If

(8)   If intReply = vbOK Then
(9)      Exit Sub
(10)  Else
(11)    Cancel = True
(12)    Me.ProjectName.Undo
(13)  End If

(14) End Sub
```

The following table steps through this procedure.

| Line | Comment |
|------|---------|
| 1 | Notes the beginning of the *BeforeUpdate* sub procedure for the *ProjectName* text box. This procedure accepts a single *argument*, *Cancel* (which is of the *Integer* data type). If *Cancel* is set to true in this procedure the event is cancelled. |
| 2 | Creates the variable required to know which choice the user has made. |
| 3 | The first of two **IF..THEN..END IF** logic blocks. This one tests to see what's happening with the *ProjectName* text box. If the contents (the *Value* property) are empty, this is a deletion attempt and the next line will run. Otherwise it's an edit attempt and program flow will jump to the **ELSE** statement within this logic block. |
| 4 | Display the message "*Delete Project Name?*" and get the user's reply. Once run, program flow jumps to the **END IF** statement for this logic block. |
| 5 | The point program flow will jump to if the test condition in Line 3 is *False*. |
| 6 | Display the message "*Change Project Name?*" and get the user's reply. |
| 7 | End of the first logic block. |
| 8 | The second logic block, here testing what the user's reply was. If they selected the **OK** button, the next line will run which basically exits the sub procedure. This means that because there was no intervention, whatever edit or deletion was made will be honored. |
| 9 | Exit the sub procedure without undoing any edits. |
| 10 | The point program flow will jump to if the test condition in Line 8 if *False*. In this case the user selected **Cancel** and we should undo any edit made to the *ProjectName* text box. |
| 11 | Set **Cancel** to *True*, which will cancel the **BeforeUpdate** event. |
| 12 | |
| | Force the **Undo** method of the *ProjectName* text box, residing on the current (**Me**) form. |
| 13 | Completes the second logic block. |
| 14 | Notes the end of the sub procedure for this **BeforeUpdate** event. |

If these two code examples seem overwhelming, don't worry. They contain a mix of *keywords* (such as **ELSE** and **TRUE**), properties (*ProjectName.Value*), objects (*ProjectName*, and *Me*), system objects (**MsgBox**), variables (*intReply*), and constants (*vbQuestion* and *vbOKCancel*). These elements are similar to the verbs, nouns, pronouns, and subjects that make up a human spoken language, and like learning a new language, we'll need an understanding of these elements and how they are used to construct meaningful *statements*, which are the equivalent of sentences in a spoken language. Each of these elements will be discussed in Chapter 2.

# Program Flow

In the two code examples above, program execution, or *Program Flow* followed a relatively simple path. The program flow began in the first example when the user clicked on a command button. The program flow begins with the first executable line within a sub procedure named *cmdCloseForm_Click()* and ends (unless an error occurs) when the procedure's **End Sub** statement is reached. In the second code example the program flow is almost identical to the first except execution begins when a user makes a change to a bound text box named *ProjectName*. A data-aware event, **BeforeUpdate** triggers automatically when a bound control on a form is edited. Thus in the second example, program flow begins with the first executable line in a procedure named *ProjectName_BeforeUpdate* and ends when the procedure's **End Sub** statement is reached.

These two examples cite the simplest way program flow can occur. It's like reading a short paragraph. The reader begins with the first word in the paragraph and parses each word sequentially through multiple sentences until reaching the last word in the paragraph. Later, we'll see examples where program flow is more complex. Sub and function procedures can *call* other sub or function procedures, thus creating jumps where program flow temporarily exits one procedure and begins sequentially processing statements in another procedure. Once the *called* procedure has had its statements processed, program flow returns to the initial jumping off point in the *calling* procedure. An example of such a jump in program flow is illustrated below.

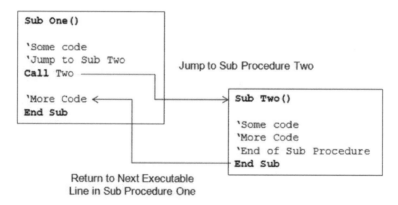

You are effectively not limited to the number of jumps between procedures, although good programming practice dictates that you organize your code to reduce the number of jumps away from the procedure marking your starting point in program flow. Fewer jumps makes both troubleshooting and understanding code far easier.

Another concept we will discuss more fully beginning in Chapter 2 is that of the *Scope* and *Lifetime* of variables and objects. These entities are essential to any programming effort in that they store data during program execution. While program flow is running through a procedure where variables and/or objects have been declared, any values assigned to those variables and objects are only "known" to the application during that program flow time. A jump from one procedure to another causes VBA to temporarily freeze the values of the variables and objects from the initial procedure and to limit their *scope*, or where in the overall application they have meaning. Variables declared in the second procedure are similarly firewalled and are only known to VBA when program flow is within that second procedure. While in the second procedure, the variables and/or objects encountered in the first procedure are generally not known to VBA, until program flow returns to the first procedure. When program flow exits a procedure by encountering an **Exit Sub**, **Exit Function**, **End Sub**, or **End Function** statement, generally variables and objects created in the procedure are erased from memory, thus terminating their lifetime. An illustration which outlines a simple of example of scope and lifetime is presented below. We mention *generally* because as will be discussed, there are methods to override this behavior by *passing* variables and objects between procedures, or by modifying the scope and lifetime of these entities.

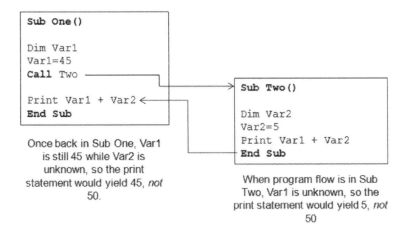

```
Sub One ()

Dim Var1
Var1=45
Call Two

Print Var1 + Var2
End Sub
```

Once back in Sub One, Var1 is still 45 while Var2 is unknown, so the print statement would yield 45, *not* 50.

```
Sub Two ()

Dim Var2
Var2=5
Print Var1 + Var2
End Sub
```

When program flow is in Sub Two, Var1 is unknown, so the print statement would yield 5, *not* 50

Because both *Var1* and *Var2* are declared in separate sub procedures, each variable's scope is limited to the procedure in which they were declared. When program flow temporarily jumps to sub procedure *Two*, the variable declared in sub procedure *One* retains its value. The lifetime of a variable in this example ends once its sub procedure ends. Scope and Lifetime are discussed more fully in Chapter 2.

## Security Issues—the New Normal

Beginning with Microsoft Access 2007, and continuing through the more recent versions, writing and running VBA code (or macros for that matter) isn't as easy as it used to be. Access 2010 ships with VBA code and macro execution turned off by default. There are several aspects to the current security model as outlined below.

# Security Considerations

| Approach | Description |
| --- | --- |
| Trust databases on a case by case basis | Under default settings, opening a database file that contains a macro or any VBA code will prompt a security warning *and* disable executable content. If you choose to trust the file Access remembers that choice for all future uses of the database. If the file is renamed or moved, the trust is revoked. |
| Trust databases based on file location | You can use the **Trust Center** to create trusted file locations and place database files there. Any file located within a trusted folder is itself trusted. |
| Trust all databases | Using the **Trust Center**, you can tell Access (and other members of the Office Suite) to trust only digitally signed files or to trust all macro and code-containing files. |
| Trust self-signed databases | You can create your own *digital certificate* using the **selfcert.exe** application that ships with the Microsoft Office Suite. Once you have attached your certificate to a database file it will open and code will be enabled regardless of your **Trust Center** settings. This procedure is discussed in Chapter 13. |
| Trust a digitally signed database | Third party vendors frequently purchase digital signatures that verify the executable code comes from a trusted source. You can also purchase such a certificate. When a signed file such as a database is first opened, the user is presented with the certificate details and must choose to trust or not trust the source. |
| Package and sign a database | Use a digital certificate to package a database file and place it on in a network location, making your database application available to co-workers for example. |

## How to Trust a Database on a Case by Case Basis

At a minimum, you will need to inform Access to trust your database the first time to create one that contains either macros or VBA code. As mentioned, this trust will be remembered until or unless the filename or its location changes.

Step 1.  Open a database file that you created and that contains either macros or VBA code. The following security prompt will appear:

Step 2.  Choose **Enable Content**. The warning bar will close and all executable code will be enabled.

Additional security issues are discussed in Chapter 13.

# The Access Database Environment

Microsoft Access is an *object* and *event-driven* application. *Objects* are discrete things such as tables, fields, forms, command buttons, and list boxes. Some objects can contain other objects, thus a form serves as a *parent* for additional objects such as text boxes and command buttons. Indeed, a **Tab Control,** contained by a **Form**, itself contains **Pages** that contain other controls. Objects are arranged in a hierarchy called the Access Object Model.

## The Microsoft Access Object Model

A highly abbreviated view of the major objects in a Microsoft Access Database are illustrated below, beginning with the **Application** object, which represents the running instance of Microsoft Access itself.

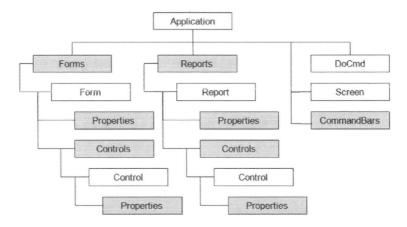

The plural nouns in the diagram represent *collections*, so the **Forms** object is a collection of all the forms in the current database. Each **Form** is also an object, and it has a couple of collections, here **Properties** and **Controls** are illustrated. The **Controls** collection for a form is the population of individual **Control** objects on a form. Each control maintains a collection of **Properties**. Also included are some top level objects that, like the **Forms** and **Reports** collections, are direct children of the **Application** object—**DoCmd**, **Screen**, and **CommandBars** are objects that are directly related to the **Application** object.

## The Data Object Model

Despite the fact that the previous illustration only shows a subset of the Access Object Model, you may notice that tables and queries were left out. For years, Microsoft Access used a separate entity, the *JET* engine (Joint Engine Technology) as the application that managed all table and query objects and presented them to Access, which served as the graphical user interface to the JET. By Access 2010 the JET is not longer used in this role and has been replaced by a technology Microsoft calls *ACE*, or the Microsoft Access Database Engine.

Like JET, ACE doesn't expose properties or methods like other objects. It does contain several *interfaces* that are objects and that mediate the interactions between both the structure of a database and its data. The most common of these interfaces is the DAO, or Data Access Object. An example of part of the DAO object model is illustrated below.

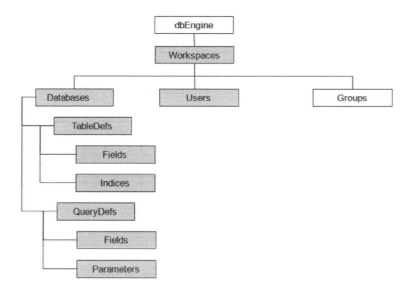

The DAO manages all aspects of the tables and queries in an Access database, as well as any user or group security that may be applied. We will work with this object model as well as another data access object, the ADO (ActiveX Data Object) in Chapter 10.

## Properties, Methods, and Events

Generally objects have *Properties* associated with them, such as *Name* or *BackgroundColor*. Many objects also have *Methods* which are built-in actions recognized by the object. The top-most object in an Access database, the **Application** object, has a method named **CompactRepair** which will compact and repair the current database.

*Events* are an object's response to some action. There are many different events and many objects are associated with one or more of them. Some events are elicited when the user clicks on an object while other events are triggered as a result of some action by the database itself. The **Application** object lacks any events while the **Command Button** responds to 12 (such as *Click*) and a data bound **Form** is associated with 50—including *Activate* and *DataChange*.

Any Access object may be referred to using VBA. Some of Access' objects are available to VBA through the *code modules* attached to forms and reports. Other objects require manipulation of the *Data Access Object (DAO)* or the more powerful *ActiveX Data Object (ADO)*. We will discuss objects, their properties, methods, in greater detail in Chapter 6. Events are the topic of Chapter 3.

## Members of an Object

| Component | Description | Examples |
| --- | --- | --- |
| **Property** | A property describes some attribute of an object. Some objects such as tables have comparatively few properties, while objects such as text boxes have many. | *BackColor*, *Visible*, *Description,* and *CanGrow* |
| **Method** | A procedure that can act upon the object or its data. | *Requery*, *SetFocus,* and *AddNew* |
| **Event** | Events are specific actions that can be acted upon by an object. Forms and reports, including all the controls they can contain, have *events* associated with them. Events may arise from users (clicking a mouse, for example), or from the application itself (moving to a new record on a form). Each event associated with an object has a small section of VBA code called an *event handler*. You use these to frame your own code to specify a procedure the event triggers. | *Click*, *DoubleClick*, *BeforeUpdate*, *Close,* and *LostFocus* |

# The Access Development Environment

Access provides developers with an easy to use environment to manipulate the objects, properties, methods, and events associated with forms, reports, and the objects they can contain. The development environment for forms and reports is nearly identical. As a developer, you'll find yourself moving frequently between **Design View** and the other, more functional views such as **Form View** or **Print Preview**. Whenever you need to add VBA code, either to a form or a report, or when you work with a general or a class module, you will work with the **VBA Editor**, which is introduced in the next section.

## Views Available to the Developer

| View | Applies to | Comments |
|---|---|---|
| Design | Forms and Reports | Used to lay out and construct forms and reports. This view gives you access to toolboxes (which contain controls), the properties window, macro builder, expression builder, QBE window, and the class module. |
| Form | Forms only | Used typically for data entry or data editing. This is the view users work with. |
| Datasheet | Forms only | Converts your form into a table view. This view displays only fields, not controls such as command buttons. |
| Print Preview | Forms and Reports | Displays the form or report as it will appear when printed. |
| Layout Preview | Forms and Reports | Displays a form or report with data but maintains the ability to modify some design attributes. |
| VBA Editor | Forms, Reports, and Modules | This is the Microsoft Visual Basic for Applications code editor. This facility, discussed below, is available to all members of the Microsoft Office Suite. |

# Code Behind the Form (CBF)

Every form and report you create has a **Class Module** that may be attached to it. This module (also known as a **Code Module**) is the place where all VBA code is stored. Because Access can handle events using VBA, event handlers (called *event procedures*) are stored in these modules as well. For our purposes, the difference between a *Class* and a *Code* Module is academic and for code behind a form or report either term can be used.

In previous versions of Microsoft Access code modules were automatically created when a form or report was created. In Access 2010 forms and reports by default lack a code module. You create a code module in one of two ways:

- Set the **Has Module** property (located on the **Other** tab of the **Property Sheet**) to *Yes*.
- Evoke an **Event Handler** by selecting a form or report object (such as the form, report, or one of the attached controls) and choosing **Event Procedure** from any event listed on the **Event** tab of the **Property Sheet**.

Any VBA programming that is associated with a particular form or report will use this code behind the form approach.

A Class Module associated with a form or report has two basic components. First, a *General Declarations* section—used to declare variables, constants, and/or objects which need to be "seen" by all of the procedures within the class module. The General Declarations section may not contain executable code. It is only used to declare specific entities. The second component contains the event procedures and any user-defined sub or function procedures. The event procedures are generated automatically. For every object on a form or report, including the form and report itself, there exists an event handler for every event the object is capable of responding to. The user-defined procedures are any sub or function procedures you create. Between the event and user-define procedures, this is where any executable code must be placed within the class module.

You access these section of the class module by using the **Project Explorer** (discussed on page 21) and the **Code Window** (illustrated on page 25).

# Modules

A second route to creating VBA code is to work with one or more **Modules**. These objects appear listed in the **Navigation Pane** under the category **Modules**. There are two types of modules:

- A general **Module** contains sub and function procedures which are available to all objects within the current database. **Modules** lack *event handlers* since they are not associated with a specific form or report. Modules are excellent places to locate code shared by two or more objects.

- A **Class Module** is a special module used to define a *Class*. Classes are used to create definitions for custom objects. For example, you can create an object named *Employee* and attach properties such as *LastName* and *HireDate* along with methods such as *Hire*, *Retire*, and *Terminate*.

Like Class Modules for forms and reports (discussed above), these modules also have a *General Declarations* section—used to create variables, constants, and objects with scope across the module, as well an any user-defined sub and function procedures. General and class modules not affiliated with a form or a report lack event procedures since they are not directly associated with event-sensing objects such as a form or report.

Technically, a *Class Module* defines an object that may be *instantiated*. This process lets you create multiple *instances* of the object. Forms and reports are both capable of being *instantiated* and therefore their code modules are formally called *Class Modules*.

# Design Time, Run Time, and Break Mode

The Access development environment has three modes that correspond to the state your application is in. The properties of many objects are restricted in their ability to be set or read during either design or run time. For example, you may only read the *caption* property of a form during run time or break mode.

## Design Time, Run Time, and Break Mode

| Mode | Comment |
|------|---------|
| **Design Time** | Design time is active whenever you are designing a form or report. For Forms and Reports, no program execution occurs during this mode. For procedures located within general modules you can test run code. See the next section for details. |
| **Run Time** | Run time is the state when your form is in **Form** or **Form Layout** view or your report is in **Report** or **Print Preview** mode. During run time your application is active and can respond to *events*. If the form or report is *bound* to a record source, it also displays data and in the case of forms, supports data entry, editing, and deletion. |
| **Break Mode** | Break mode occurs when run time mode halts. Run time halts whenever: |
| | **An untrapped error occurs**. A dialog box will appear which will give the user the choice of ending program execution or electing to debug the problem. Choosing debug will set the code into Break Mode. |
| | **The program encounters a *Stop* statement or a breakpoint** (see the lesson on Error Handling Errors for more information). Breakpoints are discussed in Chapter 9. |

# Running Your Code

Where you locate VBA code controls how and when it runs. In most projects, the entry point for your code is almost always an event handler, such as the *Click* event for a command button or the *Open* event for a form or a report. The following simple rules apply to running code:

- If you place code within any event handler associated with the class module for a form or a report, the code runs when the event is triggered and events are generally only triggered when a form is in **Form** or **Form Layout** view, or a report is in **Report** or **Print Preview** view.

- If you create a sub or function procedure within a form or report class module, the code will not run unless the procedure is referenced elsewhere. Generally such procedures are referenced via code in an event handler. Such procedures cannot be run while working in design time in the VBA editor—the form or report must be open in one of the views discussed above.

- Code placed in a general module, like that placed in a form or report class module, will not run unless referenced elsewhere in code. Again, most developers hook onto such procedures via an event handler. Code within a general module can be run while in the VBA editor in design time. If you place the insertion point within a **Sub** procedure and select the **Run** button (standard toolbar), or chose **Run** from the **Run** menu, or select **Step Into** from the **Debug** menu, your sub procedure will run.

- Running a **Function** procedure from within a general module during design time is a bit different since the procedure is expected to return a value. One way to run a function during design time(for testing purposes) is to move to the **Immediate Window** (discussed on page 29) and issue a command similar to the following:

```
Print MyFunction()  'will work if function has no arguments
Print MyFunction(99) 'works if function accepts single numeric
        argument
Print MyFunction("hello", 5)  'works if function accepts a
        string and a numeric argument.
```

In each of the three previous examples, the return value of the function will appear on the next blank line within the **Immediate Window**.

 If a function is defined in a General Module, it is also available to Queries and when defining some properties in Table Design such as a validation rule.

# The VBA Editor

All modules, whether attached as code behind the form (or report), or defined as a general or class module are managed using the VBA Code Editor. This sophisticated code editor has remained unchanged for many versions of the Microsoft Office Suite. It offers multiple tools to support code creation, object lookup, variable testing, and general debugging. All of these features will be discussed in this book in greater detail, so this section serves as a top-level introduction to the editor's tools. You work with the **VBA Editor** in either **Design Time** or **Break Mode**.

The VB Editor is a complex program-editing environment that is responsible for:

- Assembling all the projects associated with your application.
- Providing tools for editing program procedures and standardizing the display of procedures.
- Checking the integrity of program procedures.
- Providing tools for tracking and debugging errors in program procedures.
- Providing reference tools to help you understand the Visual Basic language.

The major components of the VBA Editor that you need to be aware of at this point are the Main Menu, the Standard Toolbar, the Project Explorer Window, the Properties Window, the Code Window, and the Immediate Window. We will tour these components and then briefly discuss the additional tools offered by the editor.

 The VBA editor isn't unique to Microsoft Access. It is a standard component of the Microsoft Office Suite and it is available for writing VBA code behind Microsoft Word, Excel, PowerPoint, and Outlook. What's different between these applications is the object model but all other aspects of the editor and the core components of the VBA programming language are the same across the Office suite

## How to Open the VBA Editor for a Form or Report

Step 1.    Ensure that the form or report is displayed in **Design View**.

Step 2.    On the **Design** tab, in the **Tools** group, choose **Code**. The VBA Editor will appear similar to the following:

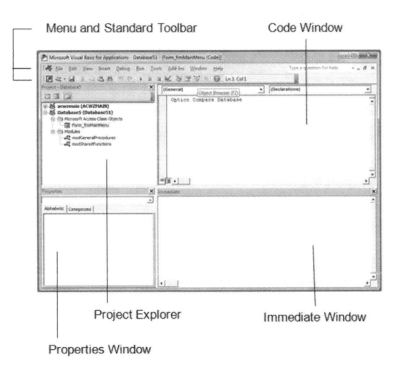

Menu and Standard Toolbar        Code Window

Project Explorer        Immediate Window

Properties Window

A more specific way to open the VBA editor is to select the form, form section, or control you wish to work with and then select the desired *event* from the **Property Sheet**. From the drop down box associated with the event, select **[Event Procedure]**. The code editor will open and display the desired event for the selected object.

The VBA editor may also be accessed by pressing *Alt F11.*

## The Standard Toolbar

The Editor tools are available through both a menu and one of several toolbars. The Standard toolbar, which appears by default, gives you access to the most important set of basic operations.

# Standard VBA Editor Toolbar

| Name | Description |
| --- | --- |
| View Access | Returns the focus to the current database. |
| Insert Object | Inserts objects such as Modules, Class Modules, and Procedures. |
| Save | Saves the current *database* with any changes to the application. |
| Cut | Cuts the selected text to the clipboard. |
| Copy | Copies the selected text to the clipboard. |
| Paste | Pastes the clipboard contents at the current cursor location. |
| Find | Finds selected text in the programming code. You can focus a search on the current procedure, module, or search all code in the database. |
| Undo | Undoes the last editing action. |
| Redo | Repeats the last editing action. |
| Run | Runs the procedure the cursor is located in. Becomes the **Continue** command if a procedure is in break mode. Equivalent to pressing the *F5* key. |
| Break | Puts a running procedure into break mode and marks the command line at which the procedure stopped. Equivalent to pressing *Ctrl+Break* keys. |
| Reset | Aborts a running procedure. This will clear any variables too. |
| Design | Toggles to and from Design mode. Relevant mainly for editing and testing user forms. |
| Project Explorer | Brings the Project Explorer to the screen. |
| Properties Window | Brings the Properties Window to the screen to check for and edit properties of Project objects. |
| Object Browser | Opens a tool useful for exploring the *members* of any object that is available to the current project. |
| Toolbox | Brings the controls toolbox to the screen. Only highlighted when a user form is active. |
| Help | Activates the VBA help system. |
| Ln Col Indictor | Indicates the current position of the cursor in the module. |

# VBA Editor Menu

| Menu | Description |
| --- | --- |
| File | Save the *database*; import or export code modules; print the current selection, module, or *project*. |
| Edit | Cut, copy and paste; indent/outdent statements; display quick info, parameters, lists of properties or methods for the current selection in code. |
| View | Toggle between viewing code or the containing object; control visibility of all editor windows; display additional toolbars such as **Debug** or **Edit**. |
| Insert | Insert procedure, module, class module, or file. |
| Debug | Controls aspects of running code; setting or removing *Watches* and *Breakpoints;* or *Compile* the database. |
| Run | Runs, breaks or resets a run time for the current procedure. |
| Tools | Establish *Library References* to other objects; set properties of the VBA code editor, and manage properties of the current database (such as password protecting code). |
| Add-ins | Manage *Add-ins*, which are installable feature set extensions for the VBA code editor. |
| Window | Arrange windows, or move between modules in the current project. |
| Help | Calls on-line help for VBA. This includes the VBA language reference, and references to the Access and Data Access object models. |

# Components of the VBA Editor

We will take a brief tour through some of the windows and tools available to the VBA editor. They include the Project Explorer, Properties Window, Code Window, Immediate Window, Watch Window, Locals Window, and the Object Explorer. Until we begin coding and executing code, the power and utility of some of these features may not be immediately clear.

# The Project Explorer Window

The organization of projects and objects within a project are detailed in the Project Explorer window of the VB Editor. The Project Explorer also serves as your main access point to procedures, either to run them or to edit them. Typically, this window is docked on the top left side of the editor.

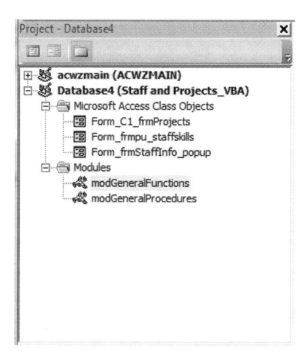

In the illustration above, there are two subfolders associated with the database file *Staff and Projects_VBA*: Microsoft Access Class Objects and Modules. The former references any **Form** or **Report** that contains VBA code and the latter references any **Modules** you may have created. Double clicking on any Class Object or Module will open that object in the **Code Window**.

The reference to **acwzmain** is a reference to the forms, objects and class modules used by Access when you work with a Wizard. You may see other projects listed in the Project Explorer as well. For example, any Access *add-in* will appear as a separate project in the Project Explorer. Depending upon the protection used, you may or may not be able to view the code in these projects.

## How to Use the Project Explorer

The Project Explorer can be used to view the code window for a particular module or object or to view the object itself. To make it clearer what type of object you are dealing with, you can categorize the information display by clicking on the **Folders** button on the **Project Explorer** toolbar.

Step 1.     Select **Folders** on the **Project Explorer** to categorize the object list by type. There are four types: Microsoft Access Class Objects, Modules, Class Modules, and References.

Step 2.     Collapse a category by clicking on the small minus sign to the left of its name. Alternatively, you can expand the category by clicking on the small plus sign.

 Projects that come from Add-Ins are typically password protected and cannot be expanded without supplying the password.

Step 3.     Locate the object you want to explore in more detail by selecting it.

Step 4.     To open the code window associated with the object, double-click on the object name, or select the **View Code** button on the **Project Explorer**.

Step 5.     To open the object itself, select the **View Object** button.

# The Properties Window

The **Properties Window** is used to view and/or change the properties that are associated with some object in a project. Every object (including forms, reports, their controls, and modules) have properties that describe the object or determine how the object behaves. These properties are set using the **Properties Window**. Properties have names which appear in the first column and values which appear in the second column. When working in either **Form** or **Report Design View** this window will display the same properties available from the **Property Sheet**. Code objects have very few properties. This window is mainly used to name general or class modules you create within the editor.

 The **Properties Window** displays properties for the currently-selected item in the **Project Explorer.** It will only display properties for those forms or reports that are currently open in **Design View**.

## How to Access the Properties Window

The Properties window, by default, appears docked in the bottom left corner of the VBA Editor, below the Project Explorer.

Step 1. From the main menu, select the **View** menu and then select **Properties Window**, or from the Standard toolbar, select the **Properties Window** button.

## How to Use the Properties Window

Step 1. On the **Project Explorer** select the object whose properties you want to review or edit. The **Properties Window** will automatically update to show you the properties of that object.

Step 2. To change a property, select the text box for the property and type a new value, or select a new value from the drop-down list.

It is also possible to change the values of a property for some object by writing the change in a VBA procedure

# The Code Window

The Code Window contains all declarative and procedure sections for modules, forms, and reports. For a form or report the code window also displays the *event handlers* for every event the form, report, and their controls can respond to.

The Code Window can display all the sub procedures, each separated from the next by a horizontal separator line (**Full Module View**), or it can display one procedure at a time (**Procedure View**). Throughout this book, *all* code examples will be illustrated in **Procedure View** for clarity.

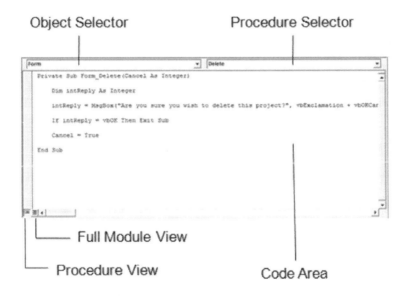

The **Object Selector** for a module that is associated with a form or report will list either the *General* object or every object contained by the form or report, as well as the form or report object itself. When the **General** object is listed, the **Procedure Selector** will either display the **Declarations** code area or list any user-created sub or function procedures associated with the current module. A code module that is not associated with a form or report will only list the **General** object in the **Object Selector**.

If an object such as a form or a control such as a command button is selected in the **Object Selector**, then the **Procedure Selector** will list all of the event handlers (also called event procedures) that the selected object can respond to.

### How to View a Procedure

Step 1.     From the **Project Explorer**, double-click on the name of the form, report, or module that contains the procedure you want to view.

Step 2.     If the procedure is associated with an *event handler*, first select the target object using the **Object Selector**, then choose the desired procedure from the **Procedures** drop-down list. If the procedure is general and not affiliated with an object, ensure that the term *General* is displayed in the **Object Selector** (or choose it if required), then select the procedure using the **Procedure Selector**.

Step 3.     If the **Procedure View** button is depressed, you will view only the selected procedure, or if the **Full Module View** button is depressed you will view the selected procedure as one of the full collections of procedures in the module. You can use the vertical scroll bar to move from one procedure to another.

 You can view multiple windows for different modules. Simply repeat the steps above for a second or third module. If multiple code windows are open, you can switch between them using the **Window** menu.

 When you close an individual code window and there are other open code windows, the view will switch to the next code window. If no other code windows are open the area reverts to a gray background. To open a code window, double click on an object or a module in the **Project Explorer**.

## Working with Modules

Modules organize your procedures into functional categories. The default module is called Module1, but you can rename it (by altering the **Name** property in the **Property Window**), create additional modules, and delete modules.

 Access recognizes two types of modules: the General module and the Class module. We will mainly be concerned with the General module. The Class module is used to define new object classes and is discussed in Chapter 6. The code modules associated with forms and reports are class modules, but they have their own designation in the Project Explorer.

## How to Create a New Module

When you create a new module from within the VBA Editor, it is stored in the **Modules** group in the **Navigation Pane.**

Step 1.      Select **Insert Module** on the **Standard** toolbar, otherwise from the **Insert** menu, choose **Module**.

 The new module will be given the name Module followed by the next available number, for example, Module2.

## How to Rename a Module

Step 1.      In the **Project Explorer,** click on the name of the module you want to rename.

Step 2.      In the **Properties** window, *double-click* on the **Name** property text box and type the new name.

 You can also rename, copy, or delete an existing module by using the **Navigation Pane.**

## How to Remove a Module

Step 1.      In the **Project Explorer,** select the name of the module you want to remove.

Step 2.      From the **File** menu choose **Remove Module.**

Step 3.      Select **Yes** to export the module as a *.bas* file, or select **No** to remove the module without saving it.

 If you export a module, you can later import the *.bas* file back into a module. You would use the **Import** command located on the **File** menu to do this.

# Components of a Module

There are three types of modules in an Access project:

- Modules associated with a form or a report. These are formally called Class Modules however we will refer to them as form or report modules (Class Modules are discussed in Chapter 6).

- Modules assigned to the Modules group (in the Navigation Pane), or when viewed from within the VBA Editor, associated with the Modules folder in the Project Explorer. We will refer to these modules as general modules.

- Modules used to create user-defined programming objects. These are called Class Modules and are considered different from the class module of a form or a report since, unlike a form or report class module, class modules associated with the Modules group are used to define custom objects.. Class modules are discussed in Chapter 6.

## Module Components

| Component | Module Type | Description |
|---|---|---|
| Declarations Section | All modules. | Used to declare variables and constants local to the module (forms and reports) or global to the database project (general and class modules). |
| Event Handlers | Form and report modules only. | Procedures to process each event that a form, report, or a control can respond to. When a new control is added to a form or report, new event handlers are automatically created. |
| User-defined Procedures | All modules. | Created only when a user specifically creates a new **Sub** or **Function** procedure in a module. |

The **Event Handlers** and **User-defined Procedures** are similar. Event handlers always begin with the reserved word **Sub** followed by the name of the object, an underscore, and the name of the event. **User-defined Procedures** always begin with either **Sub** or **Function** followed by the name of the sub or function procedure. The **General Declarations** section lacks such beginning statements, although depending upon specific settings, it may begin with the reserved words **Option Explicit** and/or **Option Compare**.

A typical **Event Handler** would appear similar to the following:

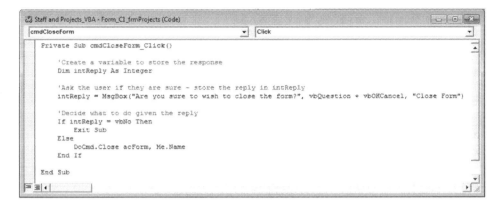

In the illustration the code window is displaying an event handler, *Click* for the object *cmdCloseForm* which is a command button on the overlying form. The code in this window is evoked whenever someone clicks on the command button. In this example, the command **DoCmd** closes the form.

# The Immediate Window

This window is used to immediately run a VBA command, or it presents output if the **Debug.Print** object/method is employed somewhere in your code. The **Immediate Window** may only run VBA commands that are *in context* . For example, if a particular form isn't open in **Form View** it is *out of context* to VBA and you cannot use VBA code to refer to the closed form. System commands and VBA code that does not refer to an object usually will run in the **Immediate Window** without a problem. Lastly, the **Immediate Window** only accepts single-line statements. Commands that are part of multi-line statements must be entered as a single line with distinct statements separated by colons ( : ). Example: FOR i=1 TO 10 : PRINT i : NEXT

## How to Access the Immediate Window

Step 1.     From the **View** menu, choose **Immediate Window**. The window will appear similar to the following.

## How to Use the Immediate Window

There are two approaches—in the simplest you enter the **Immediate Window** and type a valid VBA command. For example, entering

```
Print Now()
```

will return the current day and time from the system clock. If a form named *frmProjects* is open in **Form View**, typing

```
Print Forms("frmProjects").Controls.Count
```

will return the number of controls on the form.

The second way to use the **Immediate Window** is to embed statements referring to the **Debug** object in your code. You call the object's **Print** method and refer to a variable or string you wish to inspect. As an example, if your code contains a loop with a variable that keeps track of the number of times the loop runs (we'll call this variable *intCounter*, placing the following code within the loop would output the value of *intCounter* each time the loop cycles:

```
Debug.Print intCounter
```

# The Locals Window

This control is useful for surveying all variables within a particular procedure when the code is in **Break Point**—meaning that code execution stopped, either because it encountered a **Break Point**, a VBA Stop statement, or an error. When your code contains jumps between procedures and/or modules, the **Locals Window** can open the **Call Stack** which shows you the path taken through procedures to get to the current point. As will be discussed in Chapter 9, these are useful tools for debugging code.

## How to Use the Locals Window

Step 1.     From the **View** menu, choose **Locals Window**. The window will appear similar to the following.

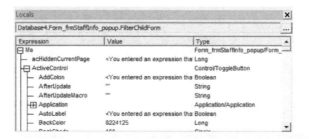

| Component | Description |
|---|---|
| Expression | This tree navigates through all properties and values of all objects that have *context* at the moment. |
| Value | The value of each property or variable. Note that for the **Locals Window** to display accurate values you must be in **Break Mode**. |
| Type | The type of object, or if a property or variable, the data type. |
| Builder (…) | Opens the **Call Stack**—useful to track which procedures were involved in getting to the current stop point in your code. |

# The Watch Window

This is a facility for watching specific variables and in this sense the **Watch Window** is different from the **Locals Window**. You can specify to simply watch a variable or an expression, or break program execution if the variable or expression either becomes *True* or simply changes.

## How to Use the Watch Window

Step 1.    From the **View** menu, choose **Watch Window**. The window will appear similar to the following.

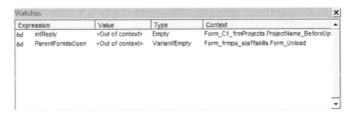

Step 2.    To add a watch, either right-click within the **Watch Window** and choose **Add Watch** from the shortcut menu, or from the **Debug Menu**, choose **Add Watch**. A dialog box similar to the following will appear:

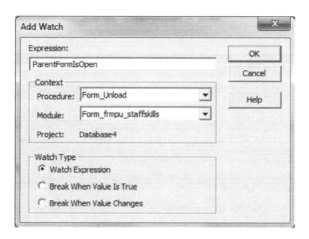

| Component | Description |
|---|---|
| **Expression** | Displays the variable or expression to watch. |
| **Context** | Sets the *scope* for the watch. For variables or expressions that are valid across procedures you may wish to broaden the context to *All Procedures* or *All Modules*, although doing so may slow program execution considerably. Best results are achieved when the **Context** is narrowed to a single procedure within a single module. |
| **Watch Type** | Specifies how to act when a variable or expression value changes. |

Step 3.    Adjust the properties of the **Add Watch** window as desired, using the previous table as a guide.

 Once a watch has been established, the effect will not be seen until you run your code *and* the specified watch condition is met. If you need to edit or delete a specific watch, right-click on the watch and choose **Edit Watch** or **Delete Watch** from the short cut menu.

 You can drag a variable or expression from a code window onto the **Watch Window** to add a watch. Doing so results in the watch being limited to the current procedure and module, with a **Watch Type** of *Watch Expression*.

# Parser Tools

The VBA editor provides several powerful tools for use when you are writing code. These tools include:

**Auto Indent**. This feature assists you in indenting code. Most programmers indent their code to show how sections of code are logically related. Indented code is easier to read and debug. Once you establish an indent (using the *Tab* key), the VBA editor will remember that indent level for all subsequent lines of code. You can continue that indent level or use the *Tab* key to create another indent level, or use *Shift + Tab* to outdent to a previous level.

**Auto Syntax Checking.** When this feature is enabled, Access will check the syntax of each line of code as you type. Although only certain types of errors can be flagged (see the Chapter on Error Handling for more information), this is a very useful feature that saves you time debugging your code.

**Auto List Members**. Many of the *reserved words* you use in VBA refer to objects. The Auto List Members feature, when enabled, will automatically list all *members* (properties and methods) of the object as you type (for example, the Auto List Members produced a list of all members of the **DoCmd** object).

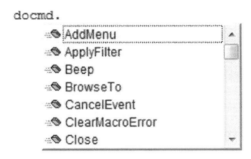

To use the Auto List Members window with existing code, position the mouse to the right of an object's dot and right-click. Select **List Properties/Methods** from the pop-up menu.

**Auto Quick Info**. Whenever you type a procedure or method, Auto Quick Info will produce a pop-up reference of the *arguments* or complete syntax for the term.

For example, the following pop-up window displays the complete syntax for the MsgBox function.

```
msgbox
MsgBox(Prompt, [Buttons As VbMsgBoxStyle = vbOKOnly], [Title], [HelpFile], [Context]) As VbMsgBoxResult
```

To view Auto Quick Info for existing code, click on a keyword or sub/function name then right-click and select **Auto Quick Info** from the pop-up menu.

**Auto Data Tips**. If your code has been placed into *break mode* (a state where program execution has been temporarily halted), Auto Data Tips permits you to float the mouse over variables and immediately view their value. The example below shows the mouse over value.

```
If dteStartDate| > Date Then
  dteStartDate = 8/19/2013
```

## How to Adjust Features of the Syntax Parser

You must be in the **VBA Editor** to adjust these settings.

Step 1.    From the **Tools** menu, choose **Options**. The **Options** dialog box will appear similar to the following:

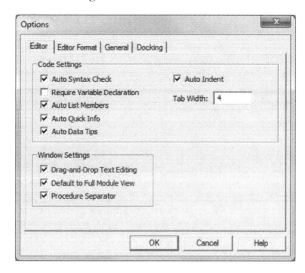

Step 2.    On the **Options** dialog box, select the **Editor** tab.

Step 3.    Enable or disable specific features by checking or unchecking the associated check box.

Step 4.    Choose **OK**.

The **Require Variable Declaration** setting is addressed on page 43.

# Debugging Tools

The VBA editor contains tools for debugging code. The overall process of debugging code is discussed in Chapter 7. In this section, we will review the debugging tools themselves.

The VBA debugging tools appear in two locations: the **Debug** toolbar and the **Debug** menu. Most of the debugging tools are used either to control program flow or to view the contents of variables. The concepts of a **Break Point** and **Break Mode** are important to debugging tools. A **Break Point** is a point in code that will halt program execution (you can create multiple **Break Points**). Encountering a **Break Point** forces program execution into **Break Mode**. This mode is distinguished from **Design Mode**, when you author or edit your code, and **Run Mode**, when your code is running without interruption (these time modes are discussed in detail on page 16). In **Break Mode** you can test the value of variables, modify some code structures, restart program execution, or execute code one statement at a time. As will be discussed in Chapter 7, whenever your code triggers an *untrapped error* your code enters **Break Mode**.

# On-Line Help

VBA has a very large number of reserved keywords, methods, properties, built-in functions, and intrinsic constants. As you begin developing applications you will no doubt memorize the correct syntax for the most commonly used VBA commands. For the remaining reserved words, most developers rely heavily on the on-line help facility. There are several ways to evoke on-line help.

To browse help contents for VBA-related subjects, you must open on-line help from within the **VBA Editor.**

## Using Context-Sensitive Help

You must be in a module for context-sensitive help.

Step 1.    Select the desired word.

Step 2.    Press *F1* to start on-line help. If the selected word is not a specific help topic, Help will begin at its home page.

## Using the Help Index

Step 1.    From the **Help** menu, choose **Microsoft Visual Basic for Applications Help**.

Step 2.    There are two search text areas: the upper left text box searches the local computer and the centered text box searches the **Microsoft Developer Network** as well as selected Internet websites. The most consistent approach to searching help will be the upper left text box as all on-line help pages stored on your local computer are consistent in their formatting.

Unfortunately it seems that with each passing version of Microsoft Access (and the Microsoft Office Suite), on-line help becomes less useful. This is a regrettable condition as the applications have not become hugely more complicated than prior versions and early issues of on-line help were similar to great programming reference guides.

## Using the Help Contents

Step 1.    From the **Help** menu, choose **Microsoft Visual Basic for Applications Help**.

Step 2.    Move to the **Table of Contents** pane (if it isn't visible, choose the **Show Table of Contents** button on the help toolbar).

Step 3.    Open a help book by selecting it.

Step 4.    Navigate through the help hierarchy by either opening additional books, based on their titles, or selecting a specific help topic.

# Chapter 2 | A BASIC Primer

Access VBA, along with the programming language for all Microsoft Office applications, is based on Microsoft's Visual Basic (VB). Visual Basic is a mature variation of standard BASIC, and has incorporated some advanced features along the way. Many of these features have been borrowed from other languages such as C++, FORTRAN, Pascal, and COBOL.

Visual Basic and Visual Basic for Applications are both relatively easy languages to learn. Although there are over 300 *key words* in VBA, many developers know 50 to 100 keywords that they use frequently (like a spoken language—how many native English speakers use *Rapacious* in regular speech?). A key word is a word or phrase that is understood by the VBA editor to have syntactical meaning in the language. Many keywords have additional *arguments,* which control specific parameters of the keyword. Developers frequently use on-line help to get details about new or infrequently used keywords.

In addition to keywords there are *reserved words.* These are created by the programmer and include all variables, constants, objects, and sub and function procedures. Once each of these items are named the VBA editor reserves the name, thus giving each reserved word a special meaning to the editor.

A *statement* is the smallest component of computer programming code that has functional meaning. Statements almost always occupy an individual line in computer code. The complex statements (variously referred to as program flow, logic blocks, or compound statements) can be thought of as rough analogs to paragraphs in a written language. An example of a simple statement is the keyword **STOP**, while a compound statement can be represented by the **IF..THEN..ENDIF** group of keywords.

 Nearly all computer languages, including VBA, permit you to format a compound statement on a single line in the code editor. This approach should be avoided as it is far easier to write, edit, and troubleshoot a compound statement when each unit occupies a single line.

This Chapter will focus on surveying the essential components of the VBA language. Working within the language to conduct specific types of tasks will be the focus of later Chapters.

## The Components of a VBA Application

VBA consists of a collection of elements you work with to define an application. Each of these elements must exist within the confines of a form or report class module or within a general module. Specifically, modules can be further broken down into two sections. The *General*

*Declarations* section is where certain non-executing commands are located. *Procedures* (either sub procedures or function procedures) make up the remainder of the module. A procedure may be built-in, such as an *event handler*, or it may be a custom procedure you created.

## An Example of the VBA Components

The following code fragment is from a single event handler, a procedure attached to a text box named *ProjectStartDate* which handles the *BeforeUpdate* event. The purpose of the procedure is to ensure that the user hasn't entered a project start date that is in the future. If this happens, a message box asks the user if they would rather substitute today's date. The user is presented with three command buttons on the message box: *Yes*, *No*, and *Cancel*. Choosing *Yes* conducts the substitution with today's date. Choosing *No* essentially clears the *ProjecStartDate* text box by setting its value property to *Null*. Choosing *Cancel* forces an undo of the data entry. Despite its small size, this example contains the essential elements of a VBA application, as outlined in the following table. Once again, for clarity line numbers have been added. These do not appear in VBA code.

```
1.  Private Sub ProjectStartDate_BeforeUpdate(Cancel As
        Integer)

2.  'This procedure prevents user from creating a project
3.  ' start date that is in the future.

4.  Dim strMessage   As String
5.  Dim intReply     As Integer

6.  If ProjectStartDate.Value >= Date Then

7.      strMessage = "The start date cannot be in the " & _
8.                   "future. Use today's date instead?"

9.      intReply = MsgBox(strMessage, vbYesNoCancel)

10.     Select Case intReply
11.       Case vbYes
12.           Me.ProjectStartDate.Value = Date
13.       Case vbNo
14.           Me.ProjectStartDate.Value = Null
15.       Case vbCancel
16.           Cancel = True
17.           Me.ProjectStartDate.Undo
18.           Exit Sub
19.     End Select
20.   End If
21. End Sub
```

| Component | Description |
|---|---|
| **Comments** | One or more lines of explanatory text that are ignored by the compiler. They are useful to document your code. Lines 2 and 3 are comments. |
| **Variables** | Named storage locations within a program. Variable names must begin with an alphabetic character. A variable's name must be unique within its *scope* (see the Working with Variables section beginning on page 41 for more information). Variables are generally assigned a specific *data type*. Lines 4 and 5 create variables, which are used on Lines 7, 9 and 10. |
| **Constants** | Named storage locations that retain their value throughout the life of the program. For large applications, constants save storage space. Their values cannot be reassigned during program execution. Constants are assigned a specific *data type* when created. Line 9 contains an *intrinsic constant*, vbYesNoCancel. This constant is of the *Integer* data type (the value is *3*). In this case, specifying *vbYesNoCancel* is more readable than specifying *3*. |
| **Sub Procedures** | Sections of VBA code that perform some task. You can place sub procedures in form or report modules, or in general modules. Sub procedures generally perform some task but do not return specific, manipulated results. The same rules that apply to the scope and lifetime of variables apply to sub procedures and functions. Event handlers and user-defined procedures both fall into this category. The entire code example is a sub procedure. |
| **Function Procedures** | Similar to sub procedures but by definition return some value. This value is immediately available to the procedure that called the function. There are two built-in function procedures. The function **Date** (Line 6) returns the system date from your computer. **MsgBox** (Line 9) takes several arguments (only the two required ones are included here) and in this case, returns one of three possible **Constants** depending upon which button the user selected: *vbYes*, *vbNo*, or *vbCancel*. |
| **Keywords** | Specific words that are reserved by VBA. These words have specific actions or meanings associated with them. When you enter a keyword in any code module, the compiler automatically converts the word to mixed case. Context-sensitive help is available for any keyword. Every term is a keyword except the two named variables (*strMessage* and *intReply*) and the named control (*ProjectStartDate*). |
| **Objects** | The things that can be manipulated, either by a user or programmatically. Nearly all objects have some **Properties**. Many have **Methods** and those associated with forms and reports (including their attached controls) also have **Events**. Although it can't been seen, the text box *ProjectStartDate* is an object (a text box on a bound form—the text box itself is bound to a field named *ProjectStartDate* in a table. Lines 6, 12, and 14 set or read the *Value* property of the object while Line 17 calls the **Undo** method. |

The remainder of this Chapter will detail these components.

# Working with Variables

Variables store data while your code executes. In the previous code example one variable stores text for use as the prompt on a message box. The second variable stores data on which message box button was selected by the user. This variable then serves to feed that data to a particular logic block (a **SELECT CASE..END SELECT** block). Any time you need to retain data for more than a line of code you'll use a variable.

Variables must have a name and a data type. They may contain a value, where the set of possible values is determined by the data type. Most programming languages, including VBA, offer a variety of data types, each of which is designed to store information as efficiently as possible. Some of the VBA data types map directly to the data types available to fields in Access tables. In some cases, there is no direct correlation between the two.

VBA provides the developer with an entire set of data conversion functions to convert from one data type to another. In addition, the data type *variant* is extremely flexible and can be used to store any other data type. Variants may be used to pass data between variables of different types as well. For example, if an imported table contains dates in a text field, you can pass the values from the text field through a variant into an Access date/time field. Access will correctly convert the data into the date/time data type.

When developing an application, you will need to declare variables. The factors you should consider are:

- Which data type best suits your requirements.
- Whether to use VBA's automatic data type declaration or manually declare variables.
- The scope or visibility of the variable.
- An appropriate and meaningful name for the variable.

## Choosing the Correct Data Type

Ideally, you should choose the data type that requires the least amount of storage for your particular need, yet fits the type of information you need to manipulate (for example, utilizing the *Currency* or *Date* data types specifically fit money or date/time information).

# VBA Variable Types

| VBA Data Type | Table Data Type | Suggested Prefix | Data Range |
|---|---|---|---|
| Boolean | Yes/No, True/False | bol | True or False. |
| Byte | Number (Byte) | bte | 0 to 255 inclusive. |
| Currency | Currency | cur | +/- 922,337,203,685,477.5808 |
| Date | Date/Time | dte | January 01, 100 to December 31, 9999 |
| Decimal | Number | dec | +/- 79,228,162,514,264,337,593,543,950,335 (no decimal) <br> +/- 7.9228162514264337593543 (with decimal) |
| Double | Number (Double) | dbl | +/- $4.94065645841247^{308}$ |
| Integer | Number (Integer) | int | -32,768 to 32,767 |
| Long | Number (Long Integer) | lng | +/- 2,147,483,648 |
| LongLong | Number (Long Integer - only on 64-bit systems) | llng | +/- 9,223,372,036,854,775,808 |
| Single | Number (Single) | sgl | +/- $3.402823^{38}$ |
| String | Text | str | Any ASCII characters. Unfixed length to 2 billion characters. Fixed length to 65 Kbyte. |
| Variant | Not mapped - very flexible | var | Any data type above. |

Some field data types are remapped to VBA data types. These include the following:

| Access Field Type | Is Converted to VBA Type |
|---|---|
| Yes/No | Boolean |
| AutoNumber | Long |
| OLE Object | String |
| Memo | String |
| HyperLink | Variant |

## Declaring Variables

In VBA, there are two approaches to declaring a variable: *implicit* or *explicit declaration*. The difference being that *implicit declaration* does not require the **DIM** statement while *explicit declaration* does. What's the difference? Many beginning programmers like the implicit approach as you create a variable when you need it simply by writing a line of code that uses it. The following code fragment is an example of implicit variable declaration in that the variable, *ProjectForecastEndDate* is created when the line of code is run:

```
ProjectForecastEndDate = DateAdd("d", 45, ProjectDate)
```

If **Explicit Declaration** is enabled for your project, the same line of code would have to be modified to:

```
Dim ProjectForecastEndDate As Date
ProjectForecastEndDate = DateAdd("d", 45, ProjectDate)
```

You may be asking yourself why in anyone's right mind would you *enable* explicit declaration of variables when it always requires an additional line of code? The quick answer is because it *saves* you from situations such as the following idiotic scenario:

```
If ProjectForcastEndDate > DateAdd("D", 45, Date) Then
  MsgBox "This project requires more than 45 days!"
End If
```

The above code fragment will never resolve to *True*, so the warning message will *never* appear. Why? The original variable was named *ProjectForecastDate* and in the example above it has been misspelled. With **Implicit Variable Declaration** the VBA editor doesn't treat this as a mistake, rather *it creates a second variable* using the misspelling as the basis for the new variable name. Any seasoned programmer will tell you that you will save many hours of frustrating time trying to trouble shoot a *logic error* in your code by not having to deal with variable name misspelling by simply enforcing **Explicit Variable Declaration**.

 The other benefit to using **Explicit Variable Declaration** is that you specify a data type for your variable. When using **Implicit** declaration VBA *always* uses the **Variant** data type. Although a flexible data type, it does take a bit more memory, slows processing down a tad, and as will be discussed briefly, may result in unexpected results.

## How to Control Explicit Variable Declaration

You must be in the **VBA editor** to use this procedure.

Step 1.        From the **Tools** menu, choose **Options.**

Step 2.    Select the **Editor** tab.

Step 3.    Check the **Require Variable Declaration** checkbox.

Step 4.    Choose **OK**.

## Assigning a Value to a Variable

Throughout the remainder of this book we will assume that **Explicit Variable Declaration** has been enabled. You will see **DIM** statements where space permits and when it makes the purpose of the code more clear.

When you create a variable, either by implicit or explicit declaration, VBA assigns the value of the variable depending upon the variable type. The general rule is:

  ▪  Numeric and currency variables are assigned the value of zero.

  ▪  Text variables are assigned the value of a *zero length string ( "")*.

  ▪  Boolean variables are assigned the value of *False*.

  ▪  Date variables are assigned the value of midnight, 30 December *1899*.

  ▪  Variant variables are assigned *Empty*.

 This automatic assignment is in contrast to languages such as C and JAVA, in which newly created variables are randomly assigned a value.

To assign a variable a value you simply incorporate the variable's name on the left side of an assignment expression. For example, the following code first declares three variables, then assigns each a value.

```
Dim intCounter            As Integer
Dim strProjectName        As String
Dim dteMissionStartDate   As Date

intCounter = 100 + 7
strProjectName = "Server Upgrade"
dteMissionStartDate = #12 July 2018#
```

Note that some variables were assigned values surrounded by quotes or the pound sign (#). These are called *delimiters* and in general, any variable storing text (string and variant data types) *must* have the stored text enclosed in double quotes. In VBA, dates are delimited using the pound sign.

The use of the pound sign as a date delimiter is unique to VBA. All other programming languages treat dates as strings and use either quote or double quotes for delimiters.

To increment the value of a variable you construct a statement that both assigns value to, and references the value of, the variable. In the following code example, the variable *intCounter* stores *2* upon completion of the final line of code:

```
Dim intCounter  As Integer

intCounter = 1
intCounter = intCounter + 1
```

Other programming languages support a specific increment or decrement operator to conduct such an operation (for example, in PHP *intCounter* would increment using intCounter++). In VBA you must refer to the variable in the assignment expression as illustrated above.

You can use this format to concatenate text to a variable of the **String** data type as in this example:

```
Dim strText As String

strText = "Washington"
strText = strText & ", DC"
strText = strText & " 20002"

'strText now stores "Washington, DC 20002"
```

## Use the Variant Data Type Carefully

At first the **Variant** data type seems like an easy choice when programming, and if using implicit variable declaration, it is the default data type. If it can accept nearly any data type, why use anything else? The quick answer is that as a programmer you should always know what your variables contain. By establishing a variable of the **DateTime** data type, you always know that the variable will contain either **Null** or a valid date. The same rule applies for every other data type *except* **Variant**. By not knowing the real data type being stored by such a variable you can generate errors when, for example, you attempt to pass what should be a number to a function requiring numbers, only to discover that your variable somehow is storing what appears to be a mix of numeric and character data.

Examples of other problems:

- Storing something like "34 September 1912" will not generate an error. To the variant, this looks like a **String** rather than **DateTime** and is perfectly valid. Attempting to store a corrupt date in a variable of the **DateTime** data type would have generated an error.

- Knowing when to perform arithmetic vs. concatenation operations on variants. 100 & 45 will yield *10045*, 100 + 45 will yield *145*, "100 Main" & 45 will yield *100 Main45*, and "100 Main" + 45 will generate an error.

# Scope and Lifetime

*Scope* refers to how "visible" a variable is to the rest of your application (actually scope and lifetime apply to variables, constants , objects, and sub and function procedures as well). *Lifetime* refers to how long your variable is available to your application during run time.

Generally you declare most variables within a sub or function procedure, and by default, the *scope* of the variable is such that it can only be "seen" by elements of that sub or function procedure. Likewise, by default the *lifetime* of the variable is limited to when program execution is focused on that sub or function procedure. As an example of lifetime, if a sub procedure declares a variable named *intCountofStaff* and at the end of code execution the variable has the value *145*. Once execution ends within that sub procedure both the variable and whatever value it contained disappear from memory.

Declaring a variable in a sub or a function procedure is only one of several ways to create a variable. The following table lists all options along with three very different ramifications for both scope and lifetime.

# Variable Scope and Lifetime

| Location of Variable Declaration | Scope and Lifetime |
|---|---|
| Sub procedure or function within a form or report's class module | Scope is restricted to that sub procedure or function where the variable was declared. The variable's lifetime passes when control leaves the sub procedure or function. |
| Declarations section of a form or report's class module. | Scope is elevated to all sub procedures and functions for that form or report (in other words, for all procedures contained within that module). The variable's lifetime is the same as that of the form or the report. |
| Declarations section of a module (accessed via the Module tab of the database window), or any sub procedures or functions of a module. | As above. Any variable or object declared in the General Declarations section of a module is accessible to all procedures contained within that module. Scope elevates to global if the **Public** keyword is used in the declaration. The lifetime of a public variable is the lifetime of the database application. A **Public** variable is seen by all procedures across the entire application. |

## The STATIC Keyword as an Exception to Lifetime

You can override the lifetime limitations on variables that have been defined in a sub procedure or a function by using the **Static** keyword when defining the variable. Consider the code fragment below.

```
Sub ValidateCountry

Dim strCountryName          As String
Dim Static strCountryCapital As String
```

The variable *strCountryName* will expire once program flow exits the *ValidateCountry* sub procedure. In contrast, the variable *strCountryCapital* will retain any value assigned to it after program flow exits the sub procedure. Because the variable was defined within the procedure, its scope is limited to the *ValidateCountry* procedure.

Static variables are useful anytime a procedure must keep track of a running total or a specific state. Any feature of your application that toggles between two states must use static variables. In the code fragment below, the variable *bolIsBold* changes state each time the procedure is evoked.

```
Static bolIsBold As Binary
'Use the Not operator to toggle between true and false
bolIsBold = Not bolIsBold
```

## The PUBLIC Keyword as an Exception to Scope

By default, variables declared within a procedure are local only to that procedure. If a variable is declared in the Declarations section of a module, its scope is elevated to all procedures within that module. If you use the **PUBLIC** keyword at the module level when declaring a variable, constant, or object, scope is elevated to the entire application—meaning that any procedure in any module within the current database file (project) can see the variable, constant, or object. Further, the lifetime of a public object now equals the lifetime of the application itself (except the variable, constant, or object must be "given life" as an executable statement in a procedure.

# Working with Constants

Constants are treated like variables with the exception that their value is assigned only once and may not change during program execution. Value assignment must occur when the constant is defined. Once defined, constants are available to all components of your application. If the value of a constant requires editing, it is done only once at the point where it was defined, but only during design time. Attempting to change constant value during run time will generate an error.

The benefit of using constants is their define-once nature. An example might be an inflation index that features prominently in calculations which appear in many places within a module. By defining the constant and assigning a value to in one location, but referring to the constant many times in various equations, you limit the effort required to change the inflation index value across the module. As described above, if you use the **PUBLIC** keyword when defining the constant in one module, its scope is elevated to all procedures in all modules across the database application.

The code fragment below defines a constant once. This constant, if defined in the Declarations section of a general module, could then be referred to in any procedure associated with that module.

```
Const sngInflationRate As Single = 0.0625
```

## Intrinsic Constants

Both Access and VBA come with a large number of *intrinsic constants*. These are predefined constants that are required by some Access or VBA built-in functions.

Intrinsic constants are denoted by their two-letter prefix, as illustrated in the following table.

## Examples of Intrinsic Constants

| Parent | Prefix | Example |
| --- | --- | --- |
| **Access** | ac | acOpenForm |
| **Visual Basic** | vb | vbYesNoCancel |
| **Data Access Object** | db | dbSortKorean |
| **ActiveX Data Object** | ad | adOpenDynamic |
| **Excel** | xl | xlChartType |
| **Word** | wd | wdFootnoteLocation |

Intrinsic constants make reading your code easier. Consider the following two code fragments which provide *arguments* for the **MsgBox** (Message Box) function:

```
MsgBox "Do you want to Quit?", vbYesNo, "Close database"

MsgBox "Do you want to Quit?",4, "Close database"
```

Both code fragments would run identically, yet the first example is clearer in that you know what buttons will appear on the message box (a Yes and No button). In the second example, the value 4 equates to the same button choice yet is meaningless to the reader.

The code editor will present intrinsic constants as long as the **Auto Quick Info** feature is enabled (this was discussed on page 33).

# Working with Numbers, Strings and Dates

Of the wide variety of variable data types VBA recognizes by far the most commonly-used ones are *numeric*, *string* (or character), and *date/time* data types. We've mentioned concerns when working with the *Variant* data type, so in this section detailed points concerning how to work with these broadly-applied data types.

## Working with Numeric Data Types

Of the numeric data types, the biggest difference between them is whether you can assign a value that represents a decimal number. The Boolean, Byte, Integer, and Long only support whole numbers (and only within specific ranges as defined by the table on page 42). Assigning a decimal value to these data types will generate an error during compile or run time. The remaining data types support decimal values and hence work with real numbers. The following examples highlight how to assign numeric values to some data types.

```
Dim intMyInteger As Integer
Dim curMyMoney  As Currency
Dim dblMyDouble As Double

intMyInteger = 205
curMyMoney = 1700.46
dblMyDouble = 45667563.44309
```

In the examples above the variables are assigned literal numbers (note that are not delimited using quotes or other characters). Other ways to assign a numeric data type is via an expression that contains an operation (such as = 18 + 77), or through the result of a function that returns numeric data (for example the absolute function: intMyInteger = **Abs**(-400) returns 400).

Note that the only non-numeric symbol permitted is the decimal point (.) and only then for data types which accept real numbers. If you require formatting, such as the use of a local currency symbol or thousands separator (these vary depending upon the local country settings in Windows) you use the **Format** function. To format the *curMyMoney* variable above into a variety of forms, you may enter expressions such as:

```
Format(curMyMoney, "Currency") ' would return $1,700.46
'If running US system settings. For systems assigned to a Euro
    country the output would be €1.700,46
Format(curMoney, "$#,###.#") ' would return $1,700.5 - note
    that only displaying a single significant digit forces a
    round-up to .5!
```

The **Format()** function is a powerful tool for formatting string, numeric and date/time data types. It accepts some predefined format masks such as *Currency* or *Medium Date*, as well as a fairly large set of characters used to create custom formats.

Numeric data types can be manipulated either in expressions using arithmetic operators (such as + / -) or via functions that accept numeric arguments, as in the following examples.

```
intNewInt = intMyInteger + 145
intNewInt = intMyInteger / 3 'returns 68 if intMyInteger=205
Round(dbyMyDouble, 2) 'returns 45667563.44 if dblMyDouble is
    45667563.44309
```

## Working with String Data Types

The *String* data type can be configured into two forms. A *variable length string* can accept any number of characters, numerals, and symbols from zero to about 2 billion. The VBA editor manages the memory requirements during run time. Under some circumstances you may find it more convenient to work with a *fixed length string*. Such a variable will be limited to the number of characters it may contain, and if passed a larger string, will crop the excess from the right hand side (in other words the variable is loaded from left to right). We've already discussed the creation of standard variable length strings in prior sections. To declare and work with a fixed length string consider the following examples:

```
Dim strFixed As String * 5  'creates a 5-space variable
strFixed = "Abcde"     'stores Abcde
strFixed = "fghijklmnop"  'stores fghij and crops the rest
```

You assign a string value to a variable of the string (or variant data type) in one of several ways: by assigning a quote-delimited literal string, by passing the value of another variable (if of a numeric data type the value is *coerced* into a string), or by using the *concatenation operator* ( & ) to combine two or more variables or string literals. The following code example includes each method.

```
Dim strVar1 As String
Dim strVar2 As String
Dim strVar3 As String
strVar1 = "Wash"
strVar2 = "DC"
strVar1 = strVar1 & "ington"  'now equals Washington
strVar1 = strVar1 & ", " & strVar2 'equals Washington, DC"
strVar3 = "abc" & 45 'equals abc45. Using the plus sign would
        generate an error.
strVar3 = Left("New York", 3)  'equals New
strVar3 = Right("New York", 4) 'equals York
```

Note the two uses of the concatenation operator. In the first instance two values (*Wash* and *ington*) were combined without additional characters while in the second case a literal string consisting of a comma and a space were interjected between two strings. In the latter case, you'll need to be aware of any spaces or additional formatting required when you add two or more variables or string literals together.

## Complex Strings

Frequently when working with Access you'll come across the need to construction either a SQL statement or a string which can be used to modify a form or report property such as **Filter**. The latter behaves much like a valid **WHERE** clause in a SQL statement. SQL is itself a language, and like VBA, expects numeric data to be without delimiters and both string and date/time values to be delimited. (Access uses a variant of standard SQL in that date/time data types are delimited using the pound sign ( # ) while all other flavors of SQL treat date/time as string data types.

The exception is that SQL permits the use of the single quote when delimiting string data and this fact makes it possible to construct relatively complex SQL statements in VBA.

The key is understanding what the end-goal is. For example, in a simple case where you have three variables, *strCity*, *strState*, and *strPostalCode* and you need to combine them into a single string for the purposes of creating a mailing label, you have already seen that the concatenation operator, plus the use of string literals (including blank spaces) will yield the desired result. So the expression:

```
strCity & ", " & strState & " " & strPostalCode
```

would yield something similar to *Washington, DC 20002*. In this case knowledge of the end result— a comma following the city name, followed by a space and the state name, then followed by one or two spaces and the postal code, drives the original concatenation operation.

Consider a case where you need to create a SQL statement to pass to the **RunSQL** method of the **DoCmd** object and you are passing a numeric value contained in a variable named *intID*. The final syntactically correct SQL statement may appear similar to the following:

```
SELECT * FROM tblStaff WHERE StaffID = 4;
```

To achieve that statement by building a string from a combination of literal text and your variable the code would appear as:

```
strSQL = "SELECT * FROM tblStaff WHERE StaffID =" & intID &";"
```

Note how the double quotes are always paired to denote the literal portion of the string—the second pair is only present to append the SQL statement termination character (the semicolon ) at the end of the statement. If the value of *intID* were 4 the two previous statements are equivalent.

If you need to refer to a string value instead, the structure becomes a bit more complex. Consider the following goal:

```
strSQL = "SELECT * FROM tblStaff WHERE LastName='Dupal'
```

If the value for the LastName field is stored in a string variable named *strLastName* then the code to construct the desired SQL statement would appear as:

```
strSQL = "SELECT * FROM tblStaff WHERE LastName='" &
        strLastName & "' ;"
```

Note here that the single quotes, required in the final SQL statement to delimit the text value for the LastName field, appear *within* paired double quotes. Remember that double quotes in a VBA statement generally do not serve any purpose other than to inform the VBA editor that you are passing string literal values. Including the single quote *within* each pair ensures that they are included in the constructed string. A variation on the previous example, but now including *two* sets of string variables might, as a final product, appear as:

```
SELECT * FROM tblStaff WHERE LastName='Dupal' AND
      Department='Finance';
```

The correctly constructed VBA statement, adding a second variable *strDept* would resolve to:

```
strSQL = "SELECT * FROM tblStaff WHERE LastName='" &
      strLastName & "' AND Department='" & strDept & "' ;"
```

As mentioned, Access delimits date/time data using the pound sign. You would use the single quote as above if your code is passing a SQL statement to another database management server that expects quote-delimited date/time data. An example of working with a date is illustrated below. The final product would appear as:

```
SELECT * FROM tblStaff WHERE HireDate < #01 Jan 2010#;
```

If working with a date/time variable named *dteStartDate* the syntax would appear as:

```
strSQL = "SELECT * FROM tblStaff WHERE HireDate < #" &
      dteStartDate & "# ;"
```

So the delimiter in this case is treated exactly as the single quote delimiter with regard to its placement *within* paired double quotes.

Lastly, as a reminder that when you create strings that combine string and numeric data, only the string data is delimited. A SQL statement such as:

```
SELECT * FROM tblStaff WHERE Department='finance' AND
      StaffID=477;
```

Would appear (working with the variables *strLastName* and *intID*) as:

```
strSQL = "SELECT * FROM tblStaff WHERE LastName='" &
      strLastName & "' AND StaffID=" & intID & ";"
```

Although these examples were formulated as SQL statements, the rules laid out are general for all strings you need to build where you mix string and numeric data with literal expressions.

 When working with SQL statements and errors arise (or you do not obtain the expected results), it's useful to place a **Debug.Print** statement in your code and dump the contents of the string you are creating into the **Immediate Window**. There you can inspect the final form and look for grammatical or logic errors. Another technique is to copy the questionable output and paste it into a SQL window of the **Query Builder** and try to run the query. The user interface side of Access may display more meaningful error messages.

If you need to include a special character such as the double quote or the ampersand in a complex string expression, enter the desired character *twice* (example: "" or &&). The VBA editor will understand that you intend to use the character as a literal rather than as (in these examples) a delimiter or an operator.

## Working with Date/Time Data Types

As mentioned, Access is the odd application in that date/time data are delimited using the pound sign ( # ) rather than the string delimiter. Most other applications also delimit dates even though all computer programming languages ultimately treat date/time data as numeric values. The delimiter is required because of the presence of non-numeric characters in an otherwise numeric field. For example:

```
04/12/1955
March 12, 1955
12 March 1955
Saturday, 12 March 1955
04-12-55   'may be interpreted at 04-12-2055!
```

These are all equivalent dates. In each case non-numeric characters are present. Most programming languages know how to reduce the date to some numeric value. In the case of most operating systems it is the number of time units (generally milliseconds but some resolve to nanoseconds) since some time point in the past. By reducing a date to some number, dates can be quickly and easily sorted. Dates treated strictly as strings do not sort correctly (01 *August* 2000 would sort after 01 *April 2000* but before all other dates like 01 May 2000!).

Assigning a value to a date/time variable is similar to working with strings, except the delimiter is different. All of the following expressions yield the same result:

```
dteDate = #04/12/1955#
dteDate = #12 March 1955#
dteDate = #Saturday, March 12, 1955#
dteDate = DateAdd("d", 6, #06 March 1955#)
```

**DateAdd()** is one of a couple of powerful date/time manipulation functions—it adds or subtracts units of time from a given date. **DateDiff()** determines how many units (such as seconds, days, or weeks) are between two dates.

# Working with Procedures

Sub procedures and function procedures are logically complete sections of VBA code. They perform specific tasks or calculations and in that role they serve to modularize your code. The rules of scope and lifetime for variables apply to sub procedures and functions as well. Thus, procedures defined within a form or report class module are limited in their lifetime to that module. Scope is limited as well in that a form or report-based procedure may only be called from another module of the parent form or report. If defined within a general module, however, the scope and lifetime of a procedure are extended to that of the database application. If scope and lifetime are a concern you should consider placing the procedure in a general module.

Event handlers, which VBA automatically constructs for each control on a form or report (including the sections of a form and report, and the form or report itself) are sub procedures.

## Points on Procedures

- Sub procedures do not generally return a value. They may, however, accept arguments.
- Function procedures always return a value. Function procedures may also accept arguments.

Creating and using sub and function procedures is discussed in Chapter 5.

## Syntax for Sub Procedures

The way in which you define a sub procedure depends upon whether you intend to pass *arguments* to the sub. The rules for sub procedure syntax are simple:

- If you do not need to pass variables to your sub, simply define it by name.
- If you will be passing variables, you must define your sub with an *argument list*. This list will include the name and data type for each variable passed to the sub.

The following code fragment defines a sub that does not accept arguments.

```
Sub ClosePersonnelForms()
   DoCmd.Close acForm, "frmSalaryPopup"
   DoCmd.Close acForm, "frmBenefitPopup"
   DoCmd.Close acForm, "frmSkillsPopup"
End Sub
```

To evoke this sub procedure you simply refer to its name in code. In the following example, the sub procedure is called from a command button's click event.

```
Private Sub cmdCloseForms_Click()
   ClosePersonnelForms
End Sub
```

A sub that accepts arguments takes a slightly different form. The sub below displays a message box and appends the value of *strUserName* to the message text.

```
Sub SayHello (strUserName As String)
   MsgBox "Hello " & strUserName
End Sub
```

This sub procedure would be referred to in code simply by naming the sub and including its argument list. Note that the list is not enclosed in parenthesis. Also note that the name of the passed argument does not need to match the declared name, only the declared data type.

```
'define and populate the variable

Dim strName As String
strName = "Nancy Jones"

'call the sub procedure
```

```
SayHello strName
```

```
'note that you could have also passed a string literal:
```

```
SayHello "Nancy Jones"
```

## Syntax for Function Procedures

Function procedure definitions differ from that of sub procedures in that functions return data. Functions are defined in the context of the type of data they return.

The rules for function syntax are straightforward:

- The function name must be associated with a data type. This defines the type of data the function will return. Functions are defined using standard type declaration as part of their name.

- Functions generally have an argument list. Like sub procedures, the argument list is a parenthetically enclosed list of variable names and type declarations.

- The function's code must include a statement that assigns some value to the name of the function. This is how the function is assigned a value to return.

The code example below defines a function that performs a calculation and returns a value as a single data type. The value is returned by setting the function name, *AdjustInflation*, as the component of the left side of the equation.

```
Function AdjustInflation(num1 As Currency, index As Double) As
        Currency

    AdjustInflation = num1 * index

End Function
```

If this function was defined in a form or report class module, it could be used anywhere within that module. If it were defined in a general module, it would be available to all modules within your application. The function would be referred to using the following syntax:

```
'define the variables
Dim Num1    As Currency
Dim Index   As Double
Dim NewVal As Currency

'populate the variables
num1 = 100.00
Index = 1.2

'call the function by passing variables
NewVal = AdjustInflation(Num1, Index)

'Call the function by passing literals
NewVal = AdjustInflation(100.00,1.2)
```

In both cases, the variable *NewVal* would store the value 120.00

# Keywords

Keywords are those words and phrases that are reserved for use by VBA. Keywords include properties, methods, and objects. Keywords have the following traits:

- They are reserved by VBA and in this sense they are a subset of the *reserved words*. You may not use a keyword for the name of a constant, variable, or procedure.
- The compiler and the parser immediately recognize them. When you complete a line of code, all keywords are displayed in mixed case (first letter capitalized) and appear in blue.

- If a keyword refers to an object and the Auto List Members feature is on (see page 32), a list of members for the object will appear.

- If the keyword is a method or procedure (including procedures you create) and the Auto Quick Info feature is on (see Lesson 1), a pop-up window containing the syntax for the method or procedure call will appear.

### Getting Help on Keywords

You must be in the VBA Editor to access VBA-specific on-line help.

Step 1.     From the **Help** menu, choose **Microsoft Visual Basic for Applications Help.**

Step 2.     In the **Table of Contents** pane, choose **Visual Basic for Applications Language Reference for Office 2010** (or select the appropriate version of Office).

Step 3.     From the list of topics that opens, select the book entitled **Visual Basic Language Reference.**

Step 4.     Select and open the sub book titled **Keywords** (to learn about keywords arranged by task), or select the book titled **Keyword Summaries** to view keyword topics arranged by functional grouping.

Step 5.     Select the desired keyword.

# Keywords as Statements or Functions

Some keywords may be used as either a statement or a function. As a statement, the keyword elicits some action. When used as a function, the keyword returns some value.

A good example is **MsgBox**. Depending upon how it is used, it is either a statement (in which case it simply elicits a **Message Box**) or a function (in which case it returns a value representing the command button the user selected).

**As a statement:**

```
MsgBox "There is no response from the printer", _
    vbCritical, "Printer Error"
```

Note that as a statement, MsgBox does not use parentheses and there is no assignment operator. When the program code is run, a message box similar to the following will appear:

**As a function:**

```
intResponse = MsgBox("Do you want to continue?", _
        vbYesNoCancel + vbQuestion, _
        "Printer Error")
```

When configured as a function, however, there is an assignment statement and the MsgBox arguments are passed within parentheses. The MsgBox will return an *intrinsic constant* that indicates which button was selected (in this case, either *vbYes*, *vbNo*, or *vbCancel*). The developer builds a *Decision Structure* to manage the appropriate action depending upon the button the user chooses.

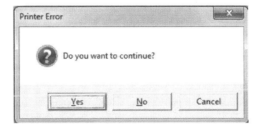

# Classes of Keywords

There are 18 categories of keywords, ranging from functions that manipulate variables, strings, and date/time values to those that make up the basic building blocks of decision structures. The following table outlines these categories and provides examples of commonly used keywords.

## VBA Keyword Categories

| Category | Description | Examples |
|----------|-------------|----------|
| Arrays | Statements that create, resize, and test arrays. | Array<br>IsArray()<br>LBound(), UBound() |

# VBA Keyword Categories

| Category | Description | Examples |
| --- | --- | --- |
| Collection Manipulation | Create and manipulate collections. | Collection<br>Add, Remove |
| Complier Directives | Create directives for how the complier will compile VBA code into an executable. Useful if your application will run under different versions of Access. | #Const<br>#If..Then..#Else |
| Control Flow | Causes branching, jumps, or looping in program flow. Discussed in Chapter 4. | Do..Loop<br>If..Endif<br>Select Case..End Case |
| Data Conversion | Convert one data type to another or pull specific time increments from date/time data. | Chr()<br>LCase(), UCase()<br>CCur(), CDate(), CStr()<br>Day(), Month(), Year() |
| Data Types | Force conversion of a data type or test for a particular data type. | IsDate(), IsEmpty(), IsNumeric(), IsNull() |
| Date/Time | Get or set system date/time, perform date calculations, set timers. | Date(), Now(), Time()<br>DateAdd(), DateDiff()<br>Timer() |
| File System | Change drives, folders, create folders and files, traverse folders, return file or folder information. | ChDir(), ChDrive()<br>FileCopy(), MkDir()<br>CurDir(), FileDateTime(), FileLen() |
| Errors | Generate or trap errors, determine error codes, control program flow during a run-time error. | Raise(), Error(), Err(), On Error, Resume, IsError() |
| Financial Functions | Calculate investments, future values, interest payments, etc. | FV(), Rate(), NPer(), PPmt(), NPV() |
| Input/Output Operations | Open, read, write, and close text and binary files. | Open(), Close(), Write #, Line Input #, Seek # |
| Math Functions | Perform trigonometry, log and exponential calculations, generate random numbers. | Sin(), Cos()<br>Exp(), Log()<br>Randomize(), Rnd() |
| Miscellaneous Functions | System commands to process pending events, run other applications, send keystrokes to an application, etc. | DoEvents()<br>AppActivate<br>SendKeys |

## VBA Keyword Categories

| Category | Description | Examples |
| --- | --- | --- |
| Operators | Perform arithmetic, logical, and comparison operations. | +, -, /, Mod, *<br>Not, And, Or, Xor<br>=, >, <, <=, >=, Like, Is |
| Registry Manipulation | Read or write registry settings. | GetSetting(),<br>DeleteSetting(),<br>SaveSetting() |
| String Manipulation | Convert strings and case, create repeating characters, manipulate strings, determine string length. | StrConv(), LCase(),<br>UCase(), String(), Len(),<br>Trim(), RTrim(), LTrim(),<br>Mid(), Right(), Left(), Len(),<br>Instr() |
| User Interface | Present a message, obtain user input, determine which object has current focus. | MsgBox()<br>InputBox()<br>Screen |
| Variables and Constants | Declare variables or constants, get information about a variant, refer to the current object. | Dim, Const, Public, Private<br>IsDate(),IsNumeric(),<br>IsObject()<br>Me |

# Objects

Objects are things that may be manipulated, either by the user or programmatically. They often have properties (attributes), methods (actions), and events (responses) associated with them. Everything in the Microsoft Access user interface is an object. Forms, Reports, Queries and Tables are examples of objects, as are the command buttons, text boxes, and labels that appear on forms or (minus command buttons) on reports. Objects are discussed in greater detail in Chapter 6.

You refer to an object and its property or method in a manner that depends upon whether you are referring to the object directly or as a member of a larger collection.

## Referring to a Property or Method of an Object Directly

The syntax takes the form: Object.Property or Object.Method. a period is always used to separate the object name from its property or method. For example:

```
txtTextBox.Backcolor = vbRed
'sets the backcolor property of a text box.

DoCmd.Close acReport, "rptBudgetSummary"
'refers to the Close method of the DoCmd object and
'specifically closes a report named rptBudgetSummary.
```

### Referring to a Property or Method of an Object in a Collection

If you need to refer to an object that is not within the scope of the current module, you must refer to its parent collection as well. For forms and reports this takes the form of the **Forms** or **Reports** collection, followed by the name of the form or report and then the name of the object. Within this hierarchy, each object is separated by an exclamation mark ( ! ), also known as *bang*, thus the naming convention is called bang syntax.

To refer to the value of a text box called *EmployeeID* on an open form called *frmEmployees* you would use the syntax:

```
Forms![frmEmployees]![EmployeeID].value
```

Square brackets are technically only required in object names if there is a blank space present. In practice, many developers enclose all object names in brackets.

When you are referring to an object contained within the currently running form or report, you can use the **Me** keyword rather than the longer bang syntax. For code running under an open form, referring to a text box *LastName*, could take the syntax:

```
Me!LastName.Value
```

 Use of the **Me** keyword is not required, but it assists in reminding developers that the reference is to an object on the current form or report.

### With..End With

VBA provides a special keyword pair, **With..End With** to work with the properties or methods that accompany an object. The **With..End With** structure allows you to quickly and efficiently refer to an object's properties and/or methods in one simple block.

For example, the standard way to assign some properties and a method for a text box would resemble the following code fragment.

```
txtLastName.Value = "Smith"
txtLastName.Font = "Arial"
txtLastName.FontBold = False
txtLastName.SetFocus
```

Using the **With ..End With** structure simplifies this arrangement. You mention the object only once. Within the **With..End With** structure you can refer to the object's properties and methods without referring to the object name. The code above becomes:

```
With txtLastName
    .Value = "Smith"
    .Font = "Arial"
    .FontBold = False
    .SetFocus
End With
```

# Code Layout

You will note from the various code examples in this manual that the VBA Editor supports layout styles. There are three stylistic conventions that developers frequently use to make reading code easier:

- Align the As keyword vertically in a block of variable declarations. This makes it easy to quickly identify the variables that are used in the code procedure. Use the Spacebar or the Tab key to achieve this vertical alignment.

- Use indentation to arrange logical blocks of code. This is especially useful when working with decision or looping structures and when these structures are nested within one another. By consistently applying indentation to related blocks, the developer can quickly figure the logic of a section of code. Use the *Tab* key to indent (once indented, the VBA Editor will maintain the indentation) and use the *Shift Tab* key combination to outdent code.

- Use line continuation to keep long lines of code visible within the code window. Some developers go further and indent the continued code as well, further improving the readability. To insert a line continuation, press the Spacebar , type an underbar ( _ )and then use the Enter key.

You cannot place a line continuation character *inside* a text string or an argument list. In the code that follows note that the assignment for the variable **strMessage** uses the **Concatenation Operator (&)** first, followed by a line continuation. The interrupted portions of text are enclosed in double quotes.

An example of code illustrating all three of these layout rules appears below.

```
Sub DeleteRecord()

Dim intResponse      As Integer
Dim strMessage       As String

strMessage = "Are you sure you wish to delete " & _
      "this record?"
intResponse = MsgBox(strMessage, vbYesNoCancel + _
      vbQuestion, "Delete Record")

   Select Case intResponse
     Case vbYes
       DoCmd.RunCommand acCmdDeleteRecord
       MsgBox "Record deleted."
       Exit Sub
     Case vbNo
       MsgBox "Record not deleted."
     Case vbCancel
       Exit Sub
   End Select

End Sub
```

# Designing for Maintainability

There are several techniques you can use to make your application easy to maintain.

**Give all objects meaningful names.** Access will default to numbering controls as you add them to forms and reports. Using the property sheet, rename all controls with meaningful names. A meaningful name should reflect the function of the object.

For example, a command button that closes the form should be called *cmdCloseForm*, not the Access-generated name such as *Command41*.

**Give variables and constants meaningful names**. Either use their type declaration character or append the variable name with a three-letter abbreviation to give you an idea of the data type for the variable or constant.

For example the name *intNumberOfEmployees* is clear as to both the data type of the variable and what data it stores. Contrast with *Nemp* or *EmployeeNo*, neither of which is very clear, either to the purpose of the variable or its data type.

**Add plenty of comments to your code.** Comments are always preceded with an apostrophe and are not parsed when your code is compiled. Include a short comment at the top of each sub or function you write. Use this space to include the code's author and creation date, what the code does, and list the input and output variables, if present.

 Regarding the last comment, some developers begin writing code as a series of comments that outline what the code is expected to do. They then fill in between the various comments with the appropriate code. The comments remain making the code easy to follow in a future inspection.

# Chapter 3 | Event Programming

An event is a response by an object to some action. Each object has its own set of events, some of which are triggered by actions the user takes such as a click of the mouse or by entering text, and some of which are triggered by actions of the database itself such as committing a data change in a field's value to the underlying record source or stepping to the next record on a form.

Generally, objects that can be bound to the data in a table or query (e.g., a text box) have many events whereas objects that cannot be bound (e.g., a label control), recognize few events.

Events vary by object, yet there are a common set of events that many developers work with. A good example is the **Command Button** object, which boasts 11 events. Of these, most developers use the *Click* event and no others. The most common events across most object types are listed in the following table.

The key to good event programming is to stick with the most common sense event for the task at hand. Of the 11 events just mentioned that a **Command Button** can respond to, one is **DoubleClick**. It would be very bad programming practice to use this event, even though Access makes it available. The reason being that no application offers command buttons that respond to double clicking and the Click event will fire even during a double click. You will end up confusing end users by trying to enforce a new interface paradigm by placing code in odd events. On the data-driven side things can be a bit more nuanced. In the section titled *Event Granularity*, we will discuss some actions such as opening a form and updating a record which result in a complex string of related events. Knowing which one to hook code to can be a challenging task, but a bit of practice and time with on line help will move you into the proficient category soon enough.

# Common Events

| Event | Object | Description |
|---|---|---|
| AfterUpdate | Any *bound* object | Occurs after data has been changed. For a control, the event fires immediately after the control updates the data. For forms, occurs only when the form commits all edits to the underlying record source. |
| BeforeUpdate | Any *bound* object | Occurs immediately before data will be changed. This event includes a **Cancel** argument, thus providing a way to prevent the impending update. |
| Click | Most objects | Fires whenever the user clicks once on the object with a mouse. For controls such as an Option Group, fires when the user clicks on any control within the group. |
| Current | Forms | Actuated whenever a form displays a new record. This includes when the form is initially opened, and whenever the form moves to another record. |
| DoubleClick | Most objects | Fires when the user double-clicks on an object. Note that if click event for the object has code, the double-click event will not respond. |
| Load, Unload | Forms | Occurs when a form is brought to the screen and displays data (load), or when the form is to be closed but before it is removed from the screen (unload). |
| Open, Close | Forms, Reports | For a form, Open occurs when the form is presented on the screen but before any data are displayed. For reports, occurs before the report is previewed or sent to the printer. Close occurs when a form or report is removed from the screen. |

# Writing Code for an Event Procedure

Although you can attach macros, expressions, or VBA code to an event, we will only be concerned with attaching code. By default a new form or report lacks a code module. Setting the **Has Module** property to *Yes*, or attaching code to an event will force the attachment of a code module.

## How to Write Code for an Event Procedure

Step 1.    In form or report design view, select the desired object.

Step 2.    Right-click on the object and choose **Build Event** from the shortcut menu.

Step 3.    If prompted to select a specific builder, choose **Code Builder**. Note that this option will not appear if you set the **Always use procedures** option in the

**Options dialog** box for the database (see the note box following this procedure). The VBA Editor will open.

Step 4.  In the **Code Window** of the VBA Editor, choose the desired event procedure from the **Event** drop-down box.

Step 5.  Construct your code as necessary. Return to your form or report.

To always use code for events (in the current database), move to the **File** menu and choose **Options.** From the left-hand pane select **Object Designers** and in the **Form/Report design view** area, check **Always use event procedures**.

When an event procedure for an object contains code, the event as listed in the object's **Property Window** on the **Event** tab will display the text *[Event Procedure]*. Selecting the builder associated with that event will open the VBA Editor and display the desired procedure.

# Event Granularity

Many objects, including forms and reports, recognize a large number of events. The number recognized varies between objects. For example, text boxes, which may be *bound* to an underlying field in a record set, recognize 17 events. Forms, which may be bound to records, recognize 50 events. A label, which cannot be bound, recognizes only 5 events.

As previously mentioned, for many objects, you will usually only need to consider a handful of events. For example, the command button's click event is generally all you need to work with in order to make a command button functional.

Objects that are *bound* to a data source, however, pose a different situation. Forms, text boxes, option buttons, combo boxes, and other controls that are used to display data from a table or query have many events from which to choose. Many developers rely on on-line help for guidance in determining the order in which events fire or the circumstances that will trigger an event.

## Example: Opening a Form and Tabbing Between Fields

Opening a form that contains controls bound to specific records will cause a cascade of specific events. Consider the simple form below, which contains two bound text boxes:

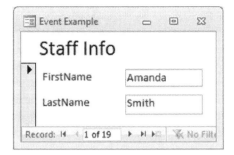

For such a form with text box controls named *FirstName* and *LastName*, the following events will occur if you open the form and use the tab key to step from the first control (*FirstName*) to the second control (*LastName*).

**Open** (form) Form is open but not yet visible on the screen.

**Load** (form) Form is open and visible.

**Resize** (form) Form receives focus (and whenever its size changes).

**Activate** (form) Form receives focus and becomes the active window.

**Current** (form) Form steps to a record and makes it the current record.

**Enter** (*FirstName* textbox) Just before control receives focus.

**GotFocus** (*FirstName* textbox) When control receives focus.

Event processing would stop here and reflects the events that fire in order to open a form and place the focus in one of the controls. If you then used the tab key to move to the *LastName* text box the following events would fire:

**Exit** (*FirstName* textbox) Just before controls loses focus.

**LostFocus** (*FirstName* textbox) When control loses focus.

**Enter** (*LastName* textbox).

**GotFocus** (*LastName* textbox).

If you then shut down the form, the following events would occur:

**Exit** (*LastName* textbox).

**LostFocus** (*LastName* textbox).

**Unload** (form) After the form closes but before it is removed from the screen.

**Deactivate** (form) Form loses focus.

**Close** (form) Form is removed from the screen.

### Example: Changing a Bound Textbox Value

Continuing with the previous example, if you were to enter the *FirstName* text box and change a person's first name, and then tab off that control, the following events would fire for the *FirstName* text box control:

**KeyDown**  Reflects your typing (either backspace, delete, or any of the alphanumeric keys).

**Dirty**  Fires once, indicating that the data in the control has changed.

**Change**  Fires once for each character changed.

**KeyUp**  Once you have completed a single keystroke.

The above events will continue to fire as you type to replace the old value with a new value. Once done and you tab off the control (or use the mouse to move to another control, or close the form) the following events associated with the *FirstName* text box fire:

**BeforeUpdate**  This event fires immediately before Access commits to the data change.

**AfterUpdate**  Fires once the change has been committed to the underlying record source.

**Exit**  Fires as the focus is about to leave the control.

**LostFocus**  Fires after the control has given focus to another control (or as the form begins its shut down sequence).

# Additional Help on Events

Against the backdrop of so many events, how do you determine which event is the most appropriate for your needs? As mentioned earlier, for many controls such as command buttons, the choice of events is restricted to a few important events such as *click* or *dblclick*. When working with bound controls the choices are less clear.

Bound control events fall into the two categories previously mentioned: user events and database events. Database events themselves fall into two categories: those events that occur before a change in the data and those events that occur after a change in the data.

On-line help provides discussion of the conditions under which an event is triggered.

### Obtaining On-Line Help on Events

You must be in the VBA Editor to access on-line help.

Step 1.       From the **Help** menu, choose **Microsoft Visual Basic for Applications Help**.

Step 2.    In the search text area, type the name of an event followed by the word *event*
Example: **Dirty event.** Press the *Enter* key when done.

Step 3.    If you are searching help based on a particular object, in the help results choose
that object. Example: **TextBox.Dirty Event (Access)**

# Working With Data Events

Data events are those events that fire due to an action involving the database. They occur for
forms, reports, or controls that are *bound* to a data source, such as a table or a query. In the case of
forms, some of these events are triggered by users, such as changing the contents of a field.

The most common data-related events are discussed in the following table.

## Common Data Events

| Event | Object | Description |
|-------|--------|-------------|
| **AfterUpdate** | Bound objects | Occurs after data has been changed. For a control, the event fires immediately after the control updates the data. For forms, occurs only when the form commits all edits to the underlying record source. |
| **BeforeUpdate** | Bound objects | Occurs immediately before data will be changed. This event includes a **Cancel** argument, thus providing a way to prevent the impending update. |
| **Change** | Bound objects | Fires whenever the contents of a text or combo box changes. The event will fire multiple times for changes involving several key presses. |
| **Delete** | Form | Triggered when the user presses the *Delete* key, but before the deletion occurs. |
| **Dirty** | Bound objects | For bound controls, triggered when data changes. Setting the **Cancel** argument to true is the same as pressing the *Esc* key. For forms, triggered when form data changes. Also includes the **Cancel** argument. |

## Points on Data Events

- Data events are generally used to conduct validation procedures or to intervene before an
  edit to data is committed.

- For events that include the **Cancel** argument, you must set **Cancel** to *True* (this cancels
  the event but does not cancel the edit). Additionally, you should call the object's **Undo**
  method in order to also restore the control.

- Data events for bound controls fire at the moment of editing (or in the case of **BeforeUpdate** and **AfterUpdate**, when the user steps off of the control). Data events for forms fire when the entire record is processed. Generally this is when the form is closed, or when the user steps to another record.

## Example: Conducting a Validation

In the following example, the value of a text box, *txtEndDate* is checked to ensure that it is valid *and* that a project start date (in the text box *txtStartDate*) is also present. This type of complex validation can only be accomplished via code.

```
Private Sub txtEndDate_BeforeUpdate(Cancel As Integer)

If txtEndDate.Value <= Date() Then
  If Not IsNull(txtStartDate.Value) Then
    'conditions are alright
    Exit Sub
  End If
End If

MsgBox "Check the Start and End Date values!"
Cancel = True
txtEndDate.Undo

End Sub
```

## Example: Canceling an Edit

In this example, when the user attempts to change the Department value (in a text box named *Department)* in an Employees record set, a message box appears to verify the user's intent. Selecting *No* cancels the edit, while selecting *Yes* permits the edit to be committed to the underlying record set.

```
Sub Department_BeforeUpdate (Cancel As Integer)

Dim intResponse As Integer
 intResponse = MsgBox("Do you want to change the " & _
        "department from " & Department.OldValue _
        & " to " & Department.Value & "?", _
        vbYesNo + vbQuestion, "Change value")
If intResponse <> vbYes Then
  Cancel = True
  Department.Undo
End If

End Sub
```

A message box generated when the previous code runs is illustrated below. The code is triggered when the user attempts to change the value in the *Department* field from *Finance* to *Accounting*.

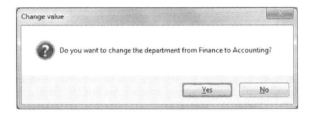

# The DoCmd Object

Controls such as command buttons are typically used to elicit some action, such as closing the current form or previewing a report. Nearly all of the standard Access commands may be emulated in VBA code by using the **DoCmd** (Do Command) object. Although this object has over 60 methods, they all fall into the general syntax:

```
DoCmd.method [Argument1], [Argument2]..
```

Many methods of the **DoCmd** object have two or more associated arguments. Like other VBA keywords with a multiple-argument list, the required arguments appear toward the beginning of the list. If you need to specify a third or fourth argument but not one of the previous ones, you use commas to maintain correct position within the method's comma-delimited list.

An example is the **OpenForm** method. This method takes several arguments. Those not included in square brackets are *not* optional.

```
DoCmd.OpenForm formname[, view][, filtername] _
[, wherecondition][, datamode][, windowmode] _
[, openargs]
```

**Example 1.** Opening a form called *frmProjects* from the current form.

```
DoCmd.OpenForm "frmProjects"
```

**Example 2.** Opening a form called *frmProjects* and filtering records to display only those where *Server* is the value in the *ProjectName* field.

```
DoCmd.OpenForm "frmProjects",acNormal,, _
        "[ProjectName] LIKE '*Server*'"
```

Access treats *Where Conditions* like SQL statements but without the SELECT FROM clause. In Example 2 the syntax is the same as if you wrote a SQL statement to filter records where the ProjectName contained the term *Server* anywhere in the field.

# Chapter 4 | Program Control Logic

There is not much difference between a program that always flows sequentially through a set of statements and a recorded macro. What makes code interesting is the ability to branch or trace different program flow paths depending upon a set of conditions that may vary over time. This can be as simple as a branch point that asks a user "Are you sure you want to do this?". Sometimes the answer is *Yes* and during other runs of the same code it may be *No*. The fact that the code can trace one path for *Yes* and another path for *No* makes up program control logic. We will examine two different topologies—branching structures and looping structures. Both permit complex behavior while serving different goals.

## Controlling Program Flow

Program flow represents the sequential steps the computer takes when processing your code. Because all Windows programs are event driven your application's program flow will be determined in large part by your users and the controls they activate.

Controlling program flow makes your application responsive to its environment. The basic idea is to present the user with a few choices and construct your code to handle the decision making behind the scene.

## Types of Program Control Structures

There are over 20 specific VBA reserved words or word pairs that control program flow. Of these, only a few are commonly used, many are relics from the old days of BASIC. In this Chapter we will explore two of the most powerful control structures: decisions and loops. There are five categories of program control as indicated below.

| Category | Action | Example |
|---|---|---|
| **Branch** | Forces program flow to another section of code. | GoTo<br>On Error |
| **Decision** | Branches based on a specific condition. | If Then..End If<br>Select Case |
| **Exit or Pause** | Exits a procedure or the program. | DoEvents<br>End<br>Exit Sub |
| **Loop** | Cycles until a condition is met. | Do..Loop<br>For..Next<br>For..Each |
| **Use Procedure** | Switches to a specific procedure. | Call<br>*Procedure Name* |

# Working with Decision Structures

Decision structures act much like the switches in a rail road yard. At each decision point they act in a binary manner. If some test condition is true, program flow moves one way, otherwise it moves the other way. For each decision point it is a binary, one way or the other, direction in flow. There are two useful decision structures: If Then and Select Case.

## If Then

This control structure can be arranged in a number of ways and represents the earliest decision structure in computer programming. The simplest form is a one-sentence structure that permits an action to occur only if a specific condition is met:

```
If condition Then action
```

If you require more flexibility to handle a condition and a default action, you would use the form:

```
If condition one Then
    Action one
Else
    Default action
End If
```

Lastly, using the ELSE IF construct, you can produce a complex decision structure:

```
If condition one Then
    Action one
ElseIf condition two Then
    Action two
ElseIf condition three Then
    Action three
Else 'this is optional-handles unmet conditions.
    Default action
End IF
```

## Example: Using If Then

On page 73, the process of conducting a validation using the *BeforeUpdate* event was explored. The message box displayed two buttons, *Yes* and *No*. In this example, the message box is modified to also display a *Cancel* button. A logic block using the IF THEN statement is used to process the button choice. If the user chooses *Cancel*, the change to the *Department* text box is undone. If the user selects *No*, the *BeforeUpdate* event is canceled but the edit remains in the text box.

```
Sub Department_BeforeUpdate (Cancel As Integer)

Dim intResponse As Integer

 intResponse = MsgBox("Do you want to change the " & _
        "department from " & Department.OldValue _
        & " to " & Department.value & "?", _
        vbYesNo + vbQuestion, "Change value")

If intResponse = vbCancel Then
  Cancel = True
  Department.Undo
ElseIf intResponse = vbNo Then
  Cancel = True
ElseIf intResponse = vbYes Then
  'do nothing special
End If

End Sub
```

## Select Case

The SELECT CASE decision structure is a more streamlined construct. When reviewing code, it is easier to follow than an IF THEN structure of similar size. Generally programmers use the IF THEN for situations where there are no more than two test conditions. They use SELECT

CASE when there are more test conditions. One appeal to SELECT CASE is that the test condition is expressed only once, with the SELECT CASE clause. The CASE statements may accept either single conditions or a list of conditions. When program flow moves through a SELECT CASE decision structure, the first CASE statement that resolves to true is processed. Following that, program flow jumps to the END SELECT statement and thus does not consider any additional CASE statements which may exist. This decision structure takes the form:

```
Select Case test
    Case condition one (list)
        Action one
    Case condition two (list)
        Action two
    Case condition three (list)
        Action three
    Case Else 'optional
        Default action if no condition is met
End Select
```

## Example: Using Select Case

The same code example from the IF..THEN discussion, rewritten to utilize SELECT CASE, appears below.

```
Sub Department_BeforeUpdate (Cancel As Integer)

 Dim intResponse As Integer

 intResponse = MsgBox("Do you want to change the " & _
        "department from " & Department.OldValue _
        & " to " & Department.value & "?", _
        vbYesNo + vbQuestion, "Change value")

Select Case intResponse
  Case vbCancel
      Cancel = True
      Department.Undo
  Case vbNo
      Cancel = True
  Case vbYes
      'do nothing special
End Select

End Sub
```

You can see how more compact and easy to read SELECT CASE can be over the equivalent IF THEN construction.

## Example: Using Select Case in a Report Switchboard

In the following example, a form contains an Option Group (named *optReportType*) that lists different types of reports. Only one option button or check box may be selected at a time in an Option Group and the selected control is indicated as a number (equivalent to the control's *Option Value* property) in the Group's *Value* property.

The *Option Value* properties of each option button (here identified by its caption) is presented in the following table:

| Caption | Option Value |
|---|---|
| Mailing Labels | 1 |
| Employee Report | 2 |
| Employees by Department | 3 |
| Project Report | 4 |
| Project Staffing Report | 5 |

An example of the form as viewed in **Form View** is illustrated below:

The Select Case statement is in the *Click* event procedure for a command button named *cmdPrint*. The code, including use of the **Select Case** statement, appears as follows:

```
Private Sub cmdPrint_Click()

Dim strReportName As String

    Select Case optReportType.Value
      Case 1
        strReportName = "rptEmployeeMailingLabels"
      Case 2
        strReportName = "rptEmployees"
      Case 3
        strReportName = "rptEmployeesbyDepartment"
      Case 4
        strReportName = "rptProjectList"
      Case 5
        strReportName = "rptProjectStaffing"
    End Select

DoCmd.OpenReport strReportName, acViewPreview

End Sub
```

## Handling Unanticipated Conditions

Both IF THEN and SELECT CASE have clauses that allow you to handle unanticipated test conditions. In the simple examples below the code is prompting the user to enter a number from 1 to 10. In both cases a situation where the user enters a number out of that range is elegantly handled.

**For IF THEN:**

```
Dim intReply As Integer

intReply = InputBox("Enter a number from 1 to 10")

If intReply >0 AND <4 Then
    MsgBox "a low number"
ElseIf intReply >3 AND <8 Then
    MsgBox "a middle number"
ElseIf intReply >7 AND <=10 Then
    MsgBox "a high number"
Else
    MsgBox "You entered a number beyond 1 to 10!"
End If
```

**For SELECT CASE:**

```
Dim intReply As Integer

intReply = InputBox("Enter a number from 1 to 10")

Select Case intReply
  Case 1 To 3
    MsgBox("a low number")
  Case 4 To 7
    MsgBox("a middle number")
  Case 8 To 10
    MsgBox("a high number")
  Case Else
    MsgBox "You entered a number beyond 1 to 10!"
End Select
```

## Points on Decision Structures

- IF THEN is a simple decision structure best suited for one or two decision points, otherwise SELECT CASE creates a more streamlined and easier to read structure.

- If it is possible to enter a decision structure where none of the test conditions are met, you should consider using either an ELSEIF or CASE ELSE block to handle these situations.

- There is no limit to the number of lines of code you can create between each IF or CASE switch point. However, too many lines of code between switch points may make your code unreadable. If you need more than 5 or 10 lines of code, consider creating a sub or function procedure (see Chapter 5) and placing a call to the procedure in the decision structure.

- Decision structures may be nested and there is no function limit to the number of nested structures you can create. When nested the program flow keeps track of what nest level it is at during code execution.

# Working with Looping Structures

Looping structures continually cycle through a series of program statements until some condition is met. In an object-oriented environment loops are often used to cycle through a *collection* of objects or to read the contents of a text file.

There are three commonly used looping structures in VBA. Their syntax is outlined in the following table. Note that optional statements are enclosed in square brackets.

| Loop Name | Syntax | Comments |
|---|---|---|
| For Next | **For** *counter* = *start* **To** *end* [Step x]<br>   'program statements<br>   **[Exit For]**<br>**Next** [*counter*] | For Next loops increment the value of the variable *counter* until counter is equal to the value specified by *end*. At that point, program control exits the loop. The optional Step parameter dictates how the counter is increments. For example Step 2 forces the counter to increment by 2, not by the default of 1. |
| Do Loop | **Do** [{**While\|Until**} condition]<br>   'program statements<br>   **[Exit Do]**<br>**Loop**<br><br>*or*<br><br>**Do**<br>   'program statements<br>   **[Exit Do]**<br>**Loop** [{**While\|Until**} condition] | Do Loops have two basic styles, depending on whether you place the exit condition at the beginning (Do) or the end (Loop) of the loop. Program control continues in the loop until (or while) the specified exit condition is met. Take care to ensure that the exit condition will eventually be met as this loop has the potential to become an infinite loop! |
| For Each | **For Each** *object* **In** *ObjectCollection*<br>   'program statements<br>   **[Exit For]**<br>**Next** [object] | An object-oriented approach to looping structures. The variable *object* must be declared as the appropriate object type for the *ObjectCollection*. As the loop cycles through each object in the collection, *object* "becomes" that object. Program control leaves the loop when there are no more objects in the *ObjectCollection*. |

## Example: Using a For Next Loop

This represents the earliest looping structure in most programming languages. It isn't particularly useful unless you are certain as to the number of times your code needs to loop. In the following example, the code forces the computer to BEEP 5 times.

```
Private Sub BeepFive()
    Dim intCounter As Integer

    For intCounter = 1 To 5
      Beep
    Next intCounter

End Sub
```

## Example: Using a Do Loop

DO LOOP structures come in two basic flavors depending upon where you locate the WHILE or UNTIL exit condition. If placed in the beginning of the loop (where the DO keyword is located) *and* the test condition isn't initially met, nothing in the DO LOOP is executed, otherwise program flow enters the loop. If either WHILE or UNTIL are located at the end of the loop (where the LOOP keyword is located) *and* the test condition isn't met, the loop runs at least once.

Care should be taken to ensure that the test condition is met at some point, otherwise your code will enter an endless loop. A confused user will have to press the ***Break*** key to stop program execution.

A common use for a Do Loop is to read the contents of a text file. Text files are opened using the **Open** keyword, and are assigned a channel number. Additional file related commands such as **Line Input** (to read each subsequent line of the file) and **EOF** (to determine the End of File) refer to the channel number specifically. Unless the file is damaged, Windows knows when it has reached the end of a text file. When this happens, the EOF (end of file) function returns *True*.

In the following example, the contents of a text box named *txtFileName* is used to get the name of a text file located in the C:\Temp folder. The file contents are loaded using the **Line Input** keyword pair into a variable, *strFileLine*. That variable's contents are then placed in a text box named *txtFileText*. Note that the constant *vbCrLf* appends a Carriage Return/Line Feed at the end of each file line. This ensures that the file's contents are viewed as separate lines in the text box. The entire code is placed in the *click* event procedure for a command button named *cmdGetFile*.

```
Private Sub cmdGetFile_Click()
   If txtFileName.Value = "" Then Exit Sub

   Dim strFileLine As String

   'clear any text from the display text box
   txtFileText.Value = ""

   Open "C:\temp\" & txtFileName.Value For Input As #1

      Do Until EOF(1)
        Line Input #1, strFileLine
        txtFileText.Value = txtFileText.Value & _
               strFileLine & vbCrLf
      Loop

   Close #1

End Sub
```

 Do..Loops play prominently in operations that cycle through recordsets. Such operations will be discussed in Chapters 10 and 11.

## Example: Using For Each to Cycle Through a Collection of Form Controls

The FOR EACH loop is specifically designed to step through a collection of objects. This is accomplished by referring to the desired collection within the structure of the loop and using a variable of the correct object type as the index item. Thus, all of the controls on a form or report may be accessed through the *controls* collection of the form or report. Forms and reports themselves are members of the *forms* and *reports* collections, respectively. Collections are always named using the plural form of the name of child collection.

Because each form serves as a *container* for its controls, you can cycle through the **Controls** collection of a form (or report) and programmatically address each control in turn. In this example, alternatively pressing a command button toggles the text color (the property is called Forecolor) between black and red. A command button named *cmdFontToggle* houses the code in its Click event procedure. A static variable, *bolToggle* alternates between *True* and *False*. The FOR EACH loop cycles though *all* controls on the form. Because some controls do not have a

Forecolor property and would therefore cause an error if addressed, the code includes an IF THEN block to only work with controls where the **ControlType** property is equal to the intrinsic constant *acTextBox*. Within this block is a nested IF THEN block that applies either black (0) or red (vbRed) to the text box.

```
Private Sub cmdFontToggle_Click()

    Dim ctrl          As Control
    Static bolToggle As Boolean

For Each ctrl In Me.Controls
    'only apply if the control is a text box
    If ctrl.ControlType = acTextBox Then
        'alternate forecolors here
        If bolToggle = False Then
         ctrl.ForeColor = vbRed
        Else
         ctrl.ForeColor = vbBlack
        End If
    End If
Next

    'alternate the static variable
    bolToggle = Not bolToggle

    End Sub
```

The reference to the **Me** object is a shortcut way of referring to the currently-running object. In this case the code is running behind a form named *frmStaffInfo*. **Me** becomes an express way to refer to the form from within the form's code. The other approach would have been to reference the form in this manner:

```
For Each ctrl In Forms!frmStaffInfo.Controls
```

These various referencing styles for objects will be more fully discussed in Chapter 6.

# Chapter 5 | Sub and Function Procedures

Chapter 3 introduced *event handlers*, which are sub procedures that are inherent in Microsoft Access and permit you to write code that can respond to user and data events. In this Chapter, we will focus on the creation of user-defined sub and function procedures.

Creating sub and function procedures allows you to modularize your code. This approach is a central tenant of all programming languages and offers the following benefits:

- Code becomes far more readable. By encasing code that performs a specific task or function into a procedure the main section of code ideally reads like a series of functional statements that make one or more calls to your sub or function procedures.

- By modularizing your code you are de facto introduced to the concept of *unit testing*. When you break code into smaller, manageable bits, you can test the smaller units to ensure that they work according to expectation. Once a sub or function procedure has been tested it is ready for use and you can focus on other sections of your project.

- Sub and function procedures allow you to reuse code efficiently. Rather than write the same couple of lines peppered throughout many locations in your application, you write the code once, in a sub or function procedure. This code then is referred to as you need in the remaining sections of your application.

## Procedures and Modules

By default, sub and function procedures created in a form or report class module are private to that module. Also by default, a procedure created in a general module is public. Public procedures may be accessed by any other object in your database application. If you need to restrict the scope of a public procedure (so for example, it may only be seen by other procedures in the same general module), you use the **Private** keyword when declaring the procedure. Example: **Private Sub** MyProcedure ().

Although procedures in a form or report class module are private, they may be called from other modules provided that the form or report is open in **Form** or **Report View**. The syntax to use is:

```
Forms![form or report name].ProcedureName
```

The common wisdom is that you locate a sub or function procedure within a form or report module when the function of the procedure is clearly restricted to that form or report. Many of the examples in this book up to this point involve procedures located behind specific forms.

When you create a sub or function procedure in a form or report module, the procedure is accessed by first selecting **General** from the **Object Selector** in the code window, then choosing the desired procedure from the **Procedure Selector**. These components were discussed on page 25.

When you create a sub or function procedure that has more universal applicability, locating it within a general module is the best approach as the scope and lifetime for the procedure elevates to that of the entire application. When working in a code window, general modules never list any other object than **General** in the **Object Selector**. Any procedure you create will be available from the **Procedure Selector**.

If you create two or more procedures, located in different general modules, and they all have the same name (*very bad programming practice!*) to refer to one of the procedures you must include the general module name using syntax similar to this example:

```
modGeneralFunctions!TransferData()
modFormOperations!TransferData()
```

# Working With Sub Procedures

The syntax for creating a sub procedure was initially discussed on page 55. Here we will delve into more detail concerning their creation and use.

The syntax for creating a sub procedure takes either of the two forms:

```
'declaring a sub procedure without arguments
[Private] Sub MySubName ()

'declaring a sub procedure with arguments
[Private] Sub MySubName ([ByVal|ByRef] Arg1 As DataType,
        [ByVal | ByRef] Arg2 As DataType [, …])
```

In the syntax above, square brackets in an argument list denote optional components. This convention is used by Microsoft and many other vendors.

## Points on Sub Procedures

- Name subs in a manner that makes their purpose clear. Further, if you are creating several procedures that work on a common object or set of data, employ a naming scheme that states the object or data first, followed by a verb phrase that describes the action of the procedure. Example: *StaffAdd*, *StaffRetire*, and *StaffRemove* are good examples of related sub procedure names that will cluster together in the **Procedure Selector** of a module.

- Sub procedures are activated (or jumped to) in code by referring to them by name. If a procedure has an argument list, you should also pass variables or literal values of the correct data type to the procedure.

- When a sub procedure calls another sub procedure, program control switches to the second sub procedure. It remains there until that procedure's code is completed or an **Exit Sub** statement is encountered. In either event, control passes back to the original procedure and execution continues from the original jump point. Lifetime rules for variables do not apply in this situation. Any variables in the first procedure are preserved while the second procedure's code is run.

- You can nest calls to procedures within procedures essentially without limit. In practice, it is not a good idea to nest calls too much because tracing errors and program logic becomes difficult.

- Sub and Function procedures support *recursion*, a sophisticated technique wherein a procedure may call itself.

## How to Create a Sub Procedure without Arguments

Step 1.     Position the insertion point *outside* an existing sub or function procedure.

Step 2.     Type the reserved word **Sub** followed by the name of your procedure.

Step 3.     Press the ***Enter*** key to complete the task of defining your procedure. The VBA editor will create a procedure and add the **End Sub** statement.

Step 4.     Create the code for your procedure.

## How to Create a Sub Procedure with Arguments

Step 1.     Position the insertion point *outside* an existing sub or function procedure.

Step 2.     Type the reserved word **Sub** followed by the name of your procedure.

Step 3.  Type a left parenthesis, the name of the first argument, the As keyword, and a variable type. Continue with additional arguments as required, keeping each argument separated by a comma. Complete the argument list when done by typing a right parenthesis. Press the **Enter** key when done.

Step 4.  Create the code for your procedure.

 If you begin a sub or function procedure with the reserved word **Private** the scope for the procedure will become local to its parent module.

## Passing Arguments: ByVal or ByRef

By default, VBA passes arguments *By Reference*. If you need to pass an argument *By Value* begin each argument assignment with the reserved word **ByVal**. Alternatively, if you wish your argument list to be clear regarding how arguments are passed, begin each argument assignment using either **ByVal** or **ByRef**.

When a variable is passed *By Reference*, the value of the variable may be changed in other sub or function procedures. Take a look at the following graphic.

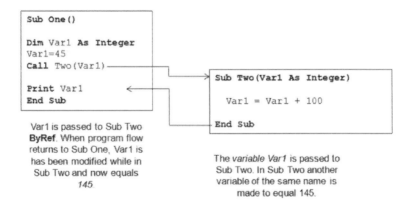

```
Sub One()

Dim Var1 As Integer
Var1=45
Call Two(Var1)

Print Var1
End Sub
```

Var1 is passed to Sub Two **ByRef**. When program flow returns to Sub One, Var1 is has been modified while in Sub Two and now equals 145.

```
Sub Two(Var1 As Integer)

    Var1 = Var1 + 100

End Sub
```

The *variable Var1* is passed to Sub Two. In Sub Two another variable of the same name is made to equal 145.

The variable *Var1*, being passed to and modified within sub procedure *Two* , is now equal to the value 145 when tested back in sub procedure *One*.

When you pass an argument **ByVal**, VBA essentially makes a copy of the argument (as if the variable is passed as a literal and not a variable). The variable or value from the *calling* procedure isn't changed. Consider the following illustration.

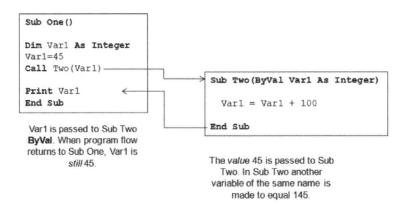

```
Sub One()

Dim Var1 As Integer
Var1=45
Call Two(Var1)

Print Var1
End Sub
```

```
Sub Two(ByVal Var1 As Integer)

    Var1 = Var1 + 100

End Sub
```

Var1 is passed to Sub Two **ByVal**. When program flow returns to Sub One, Var1 is *still* 45.

The *value* 45 is passed to Sub Two. In Sub Two another variable of the same name is made to equal 145.

A variable, *Var1* is defined in sub procedure *One* and stores the value 45. That *value*, and not a reference to the variable *Var1* is passed to sub procedure *Two* where 100 is added to it. In sub procedure *Two*, *Var1* has the value 145. When program flow returns to sub procedure *One*, everything in sub procedure *Two* loses both scope and focus. Back in sub procedure *One*, *Var1* still maintains its original value of 45.

## Calling a Sub Procedure

You call a sub procedure by referring to its name in a VBA statement. Alternatively you can use the reserved word **Call** to clearly denote that the statement is a call to a sub procedure. If your procedure is located within a general module, you may also append the module name to the sub procedure name, separated with an period (this is object oriented syntax—the procedure is considered a child of the module). The following statements calling a sub procedure named *MyProcedure* are equivalent:

```
MyProcedure
Call MyProcedure
modGeneralProcedures.MyProcedure
Call modGeneralProcedures.MyProcedure
```

When you call a sub procedure that contains one or more arguments, as you type the sub procedure name, the VBA editor will display an **auto quick info** bar that lists the arguments and their expected data types (refer to the illustration on page 33 for a refresher on **auto quick info**).

You can pass arguments by using variables or *literals*. If you pass by *literal* then any **ByRef** references do not take effect since you are not passing a variable. For a sub procedure defined as:

```
Sub ExportData (strTableName As String, numRows As Integer)
```

The following calls are equivalent:

```
ExportData strTableToExport, intMaxRows
ExportData strTableToExport, 1000
ExportData "tblStaffInformation", 500
ExportData "tblStaffInformation", intMaxRows
```

The use of **Call** or referencing to the parent module as a prefix are the same as in the previous examples.

## Exiting a Sub Procedure

The most common way to exit a sub procedure is to simply allow the full set of statements in the procedure to execute. When program flow encounters the **End Sub** statement, flow returns to the calling procedure.

There are situations however when you may want to leave the sub procedure in mid execution. The reserved word pair **Exit Sub** is used for this situation and its use is illustrated in the following code example.

```
Sub PrintArchive()
  Dim intReply As Integer

  intReply = MsgBox("The archive is large. Are you " & _
    "sure you want to print?", vbYesNo & vbQuestion)

Select Case intReply
  Case vbNo
    Exit Sub
  Case vbYes
    'you asked for it!
    DoCmd.OpenReport "rptArchive", acViewNormal
End Select

End Sub
```

# Working With Functions

Much of what has been discussed for sub procedures applies to function procedures as well. This includes the discussion on passing argument values **ByRef** or **ByVal**.

A central difference between sub and function procedures is that function procedures *always* return a value. Therefore you do not use the **Call** keyword to reference a function procedure, instead you assign the return value of the function procedure to a variable.

The general syntax for creating a function procedure was discussed on page 57. The more detailed syntax for their creation takes either of these forms:

```
'declaring a function procedure without arguments
[Private] Function MyFunction () As DataType

'declaring a function procedure with arguments
[Private] Function MyFunction ([ByVal|ByRef] Arg1 As DataType,
      [ByVal | ByRef] Arg2 As DataType [, …]) As DataType
```

Every function declaration should end in a statement that defines the data type the function will return. If you do not declare the data type VBA will return function data as the data type **Variant**. Issues regarding the use of variants is explored on page 46.

## Points on Function Procedures

- Name functions in a manner that makes their purpose clear. Because most functions also accept arguments, it is a good idea to name the arguments in an equally clear manner. The argument list will appear as an Auto Quick Info box (see page 33) when you are in the VBA Editor and type the function name.

- If a function procedure is declared within a form or report module, it is by default *Private* to that module. Placing the function procedure in a general module elevates the scope and lifetime to that of the entire application.

- Functions may call other sub or function procedures. The sub procedure nesting rules apply to functions, too.

## How to Create a Function Procedure without Arguments

Step 1.     Position the insertion point *outside* an existing sub or function procedure.

Step 2.     Type the reserved word **Function** followed by the name of your procedure.

Step 3.     Continue by typing an empty set of parenthesis (), then type the reserved word **As** and type a valid data type. Press ***Enter*** when done.

Step 4.     Create the code for your procedure. Remember that you must include an *assignment statement* that references your function name and uses the ***equal sign*** (=) to assign some value.

You may be thinking why would you create a function procedure without arguments? The following code fragment is a useful example of a function that generates a unique number (although not random) each time the function is called. It returns the number of seconds passed since 01 January 1900.

```
Function TimeStamp() As Double
    TimeStamp = DateDiff("s", #1/1/1900#, Now())
End Function
```

## How to Create a Function Procedure with Arguments

Step 1.     Position the insertion point *outside* an existing sub or function procedure.

Step 2.     Type the reserved word **Sub** followed by the name of your procedure.

Step 3.     Type a left parenthesis, the name of the first argument, the As keyword, and a variable type. Continue with additional arguments as required, keeping each argument separated by a comma. Complete the argument list when done by typing a right parenthesis.

Step 4.     Continue the definition by typing the reserved word **As** and entering in a data type for the return value of the function. Press the *Enter* key when done.

Step 5.     Create the code for your procedure. Remember that you must include an *assignment statement* that references your function name and uses the *equal sign* (=) to assign some value.

The following code example passes an array of the **Variant** data type. It returns an **Integer** value representing the number of members of the array that contain data (in other words, are not **Empty**). The first test is to ensure that the array has been defined to store more than zero members. If this is *True*, the function returns -1, otherwise it returns the number of non-empty members within the array.

```
Function ArrayCount(strArray() As Variant) As Integer
    If UBound(strArray) > 0 Then
        Dim strMember As Variant
        Dim intCount As Integer
        For Each strMember In strArray
            If Not IsEmpty(strMember) Then
                intCount = intCount + 1
            End If
        Next
        ArrayCount = intCount
    Else
        ArrayCount = -1
    End If
End Function
```

## Calling a Function Procedure

Function procedures are activated (or jumped to) in code when they are referred to as part of an assignment (or if you refer to a function using the **Debug.Print** method). If you are working with a function named *AddNumbers* that accepts two arguments, *Num1* and *Num2*, and returns the sum of these arguments, the three ways in which this function could be activated are illustrated below:

```
'assignment to another variable
Dim intTotal As Integer
intTotal = AddNumbers(10, 130)

'as a test in a condition statement
If AddNumbers (10, 130) = 140 then Exit Sub

'as a method of the Debug object
Debug.Print AddNumbers (10, 130)

'the following would however raise an error:
AddNumbers (10, 130)
```

## Example: Creating a Function Procedure that Determines if a Form is Currently Loaded

There are situations where it would be useful to know in advance whether a particular form is presently open. An example is when a form or a report requires some information from another form. In this case, it would be wise to prevent the secondary form or the report from opening if the primary form is not already open.

Here are some points to consider:

- Access lacks the direct functionality to determine the state of a form. This is in part because the Forms collection in Access refers only to forms that are currently open, either in Design View or in Form View. Attempting to refer to a form in the Forms collection that is not open in either view will generate an error.

- When a form is open, you can use the Forms collection to read the **CurrentView** property. When **CurrentView** is zero, the form is open in **Design View**. When **CurrentView** is one, the form is open in **Form View**.

- Access maintains another collection, **AllForms**, which is part of the **CurrentProject** object. This collection does permit you to reference all open or closed forms. Open forms have their **IsLoaded** property set to True, although you cannot differentiate between forms open in Form View or Design View using this collection.

- Therefore, the optimal approach is to use both collections. Cycle through the AllForms collection and for any form open, step into the Forms collection and test its CurrentView property. For any open form with a CurrentView equal to 1, the form is open in Form View.

```
Function isFormOpen(strFormName As String) As Boolean
Dim obj As AccessObject
For Each obj In CurrentProject.AllForms
   If obj.IsLoaded = True Then
    If Forms(obj.Name).CurrentView = 1 Then
      If obj.Name = strFormName Then
       isFormOpen = True
       Exit Function
      End If
    End If
   End If
Next obj
isFormOpen = False
End Function
```

The utility of this function becomes apparent when it is used in the Open event procedure of form or a report. If the form or report's operation is dependent upon some other form being opened first, the following code would prevent the secondary form or a report from opening unless the first form, here named *frmPrintSwitchboard*, is already open.

```
Private Sub Report_Open(Cancel As Integer)

If Not isFormOpen("frmPrintSwitchboard") Then
  MsgBox "The Print Switchboard form must " & _
      "be open in order to view " & _
      "or print this report.", _
      vbExclamation, "Report Error"
  Cancel = True
End If

End Sub
```

If the intent is to only use a function such as *isFormOpen* from a specific report or other object, you should consider locating it within that object's module. Otherwise, if the function has some broader utility purpose, consider placing it in a general module.

# Chapter 6 | Objects

Object-Oriented Programming, or *OOP*, has been a tremendously successful programming model and the fact that objects are pervasive in VBA underscores the power of this approach. The illustrations of the Access object model (page 11) and the Data Access Object (DAO) model (page 12) are but tiny glimpses into the true nature of these object models. Nearly *everything* in Microsoft Access is an object and can be manipulated programmatically using VBA code. The separate DAO model provides objects, methods, and properties for full manipulation of the tables, relational joins, and queries that make up an Access database. As we will see in this Chapter, using VBA you can create your own custom objects by working with Class Modules.

Technically, a programming object is simply memory space that can be referred to by name. In this simple regard an object is like a variable, although some programmers would not associate variables as objects. An object is always a member of a *Class*, which is a definition of the object. In the real world you can think of a particular model of car being produced on an assembly line. The object is the physical car being created. The *Class* for the car constitutes the blueprints and assembly instructions required to create the actual car. This is pretty apparent when you create your own objects which we will introduce shortly.

Objects generally include *methods* and *properties*. A method is a built-in action associated with the object. A property is an attribute (read/write or read-only) of the object. Thus a form in Access recognizes the **Undo** method, which restores all data on the current record to its unedited state. Like other keywords and functions in VBA, many object methods have an argument list. A common property of a form is **Caption** which is read/write. You set or read the caption property using the following syntax (here we are using the **Me** keyword which works to refer to the current form (or report) when the code is running behind the form (or report) in question:

```
'setting the caption property
Me.Caption = "Employee Information"
'reading the caption property
strCaption = Me.Caption
```

Many of the user-interface objects in Access, such as forms, reports, and their associated controls, also recognize *events*. Events were introduced in Chapter 3. Some objects such as forms and reports, are capable of responding to numerous events while other objects (typically unbound controls) may respond to only a few. You can create custom events for objects you create as well, although such events must always be initiated in code and most VBA programmers skip the extra steps and simply use procedures.

## Libraries and the Object Model

In the world of Microsoft Windows, applications that consist of objects store information about their objects in an object *library*. For many applications you will not need to reference other libraries as every Microsoft Access database file has the **Microsoft Access Object Library** automatically attached. If the project permits VBA code then the **Visual Basic for Applications Object Library** is also included.

As will be discussed in Chapter 7 (specifically when working with the **FileDialog** object), in Chapter 10 (The ADO and DAO data access objects), and in Chapter 12, (Automation) you will need to include a reference to one or more additional libraries. This is done via the **References** dialog and is accessed while in the VBA editor from the **Tools** menu.

# Creating a User Defined Object

Perhaps the best way to understand the power of objects is to first study how to create one. There are many reasons why you may want to create a custom object. The power in working with objects comes from their encapsulation of the messy programming details. Once the details of the methods and properties of a custom object have been worked out and coded, using the object in day to day programming becomes an easy task.

As an example, imagine a large organization that has formalized the process of adding a new staff member. Many departments are affected by this addition: Human Resources triggers all sorts of activity, Facilities is involved to assign a new office location, phone number, etc., while the Information Technology Department is responsible for creating user accounts, email addresses, and granting certain permissions to some information systems. In an object-oriented world such a complex background could have a front-end that was as simple as the following code fragment:

```
Dim emp As NewEmployee
Set emp = New NewEmployee
emp.FirstName = "Tonya"
emp.LastName = "Johnson"
emp.AssignID
emp.CreateEmployee
```

We will not go into the fine detail about how each process is achieved (indeed, much of this type of activity is perfect for DAO or ADO programming and will be introduced in Chapter 10). But we will create some properties and methods for a user-defined class named **NewEmployee** to illustrate how capturing much of a complex process can be turned into a relatively simple interface.

## About the Class Module

You start a new class by inserting a new **class module** while in the VBA editor. This module will closely resemble a general module, or that associated with a form or a report, but with a few exemptions.

- A property of the class is created by working with special **Property Let** and **Property Get** procedures in the class module. For read/write properties you'll create both **Property Let** (write) and **Property Get** (read) procedures. If you need a read-only property then you only create a **Property Get** procedure. Working variables used to share data between **Property Let** and **Property Get** procedures are defined within the class module's **General Declarations** section.

- Any **Sub or Function Procedure** defined in the **class module** becomes a **method** of the class.

- The **Object Selector** will only list two objects: **General** and **Class**. The **General** object will behave similarly to the **General** area in any other code window (for example it will list the **Declarations** section as well as any procedures you create). The **Class** object will only list two event handlers: **Initialize** and **Terminate**. These special events are triggered whenever an instance of your class (that is to say a *new* object of your class) is created or destroyed. In this context losing scope is a destructive event.

## How to Create a Class

You begin creating a new object by defining its class. This involves the creation of a class module.

Step 1.    From within the VBA code editor, from the **Insert** menu, choose **Class Module**.

Step 2.    To name your new class, in the **Properties Window** modify the **Name** property by typing a new class name. (In the following examples we are working with a class module named *NewEmployee*.)

 Your class name should be descriptive and reflect its general nature. Remember that the class will serve as a template for any objects you create from it and that the individual objects will have a separate and hopefully descriptive name as well. The difference between the two objects is that the class is associated with your application and should be considered a permanent object, while any objects created from your class are temporary and have limited lifetimes.

If the **Properties Window** isn't visible, press **Alt + F4** or from the **View** menu, choose **Properties Window**.

Once your class has been created and named, you create the properties and methods of that class, as well as code any actions which may be required for the class **Initialize** and **Terminate** events.

## How to Create a Property of a Class

If you require a read/write property you frequently need to also create an internal variable that can be accessed by both the **Property Let** and **Property Get** procedures for your property. Thus you first define a private variable in the **General Declarations** section of the class module. The variable name should not equal the final property name—that definition becomes part of the **Property Get** and/or **Property Let** statements.

To create a property that returns a value, you must define a **Property Get** procedure. Being able to write to a property requires a **Property Let** procedure. These procedures will be discussed separately.

Step 1.    If you are not within the **General Declarations** section of the class module, use the **Object** and **Procedures** selectors at the top of the code window to move to that area.

Step 2.    Create a property by issuing a statement using the following form:

```
Private PropertyName As Data Type
```

For example, to create a property named *FirstName* of the *NewEmployee* class, the **General Declarations** section would appear as:

```
Private strFirstName As String
```

For the following examples, the *NewEmployee* class will contain three properties: *FirstName*, *LastName*, and *EmployeeID*. The latter property will become a read-only property. In order to manipulate these properties, working variables should be created in the **General Declarations** section of the *NewEmployee* class module. In the example we're building it would appear as:

```
Private strFirstName    As String
Private strLastName     As String
Private dblEmpID        As Double
```

## How to Create a Readable Property

The **Property Get** procedure is where the property formally gets assigned a name as the name of the procedure *becomes* the name of the property. The value passed to the property within this procedure is contained within one of the working variables created in the previous procedure. In the case of a read-only property (which we will cover shortly), there will be no corresponding **Property Let** procedure. For read/write properties each property must have a **Property Get** and **Property Let** procedure. For the moment, don't worry that the working variables haven't been assigned any value. That occurs with **Property Let** procedures, or in the case of a read-only property, elsewhere in the class module.

Step 1.     Move to the bottom of the **General Procedures** section, or if you are within a sub or function procedure in the class module, position the insertion point outside of any code blocks (these could be either Sub..End Sub, Function..End Function, or Public Property.. End Property blocks).

Step 2.     Define the property using the following syntax:

```
Public Property Get PropertyName() As Data Type
```

Step 3.     Press the *Enter* key. The VBA editor will stub out the **Property Get** procedure by including an **End Property** statement.

Step 4.     At a minimum, create an assignment statement within the procedure using name of the property you just created and assigning it the value of the variable you defined in the **General Declarations** section. For example, to create a readable property named *FirstName* and working with a variable created in the class module **General Declarations** section named *strFirstName* your procedure would appear as:

```
Public Property Get FirstName() As String
    FirstName = strFirstName
End Property
```

To create the three readable properties for the *NewEmployee* class module, the three **Property Get** procedures would appear as:

```
Public Property Get FirstName() As String
    FirstName = strFirstName
End Property

Public Property Get LastName() As String
    LastName = strLastName
End Property

Public Property Get EmployeeID() As Double
    EmployeeID = dblEmpID
End Property
```

## How to Create a Writable Property

In the example we are following, only two of the properties: *FirstName* and *LastName* will be writable—that is to say, you can assign a value to the property once you have created an object based on the *NewEmployee* class. We'll address the read-only *EmployeeID* property when discussing how to create a **Method** for the new class.

Step 1.    Follow Step 1 from the previous procedure to ensure you are not within an existing code block.

Step 2.    Define the writeable attribute of the property using the following syntax:

```
Public Property Let PropertyName(ValueName As Data Type)
```

Step 3.    Press the **Enter** key. The VBA editor will stub out the **Property Let** procedure by including an **End Property** statement.

> **Warning**: The *PropertyName* value **must** be the same as the *PropertyName* value used to create the corresponding **Property Get** statement.

Step 4.    At a minimum, create an assignment statement within the procedure using the name of the variable you defined in the **General Declarations** section for this property and assigning it the name of the variable passed through the **Property Let** argument list. For example, to write to the property named *FirstName* and working with a variable created in the class module **General Declarations** section and named *strFirstName* your procedure would appear as:

```
Public Property Let FirstName(FirstName As String)
    strFirstName = FirstName
End Property
```

In this example, note that the variable created in the **General Declarations** section, which is private to this class module, is being assigned a value passed as an argument to the **Property Let** procedure. Here, for simplicity both the property name and the variable passed via the argument list are the same. This isn't required and if you changed the variable *FirstName* both in the argument list definition and in the code to something like *NewValue* the code will still run as expected. The second **Property Let** procedure below proves the point.

To create the two writable properties for the *NewEmployee* class module, the two **Property Let** procedures would appear as:

```
Public Property Let FirstName(FirstName As String)
    strFirstName = FirstName
End Property

Public Property Let LastName(strLastName1 As String)
    strLastName = strLastName1
End Property
```

## How to Create a Read-Only Property

A read-only property has a **Property Get** procedure in order to read the property value, but lacks the corresponding **Property Let** procedure. You must ensure that the property is somehow assigned and there are two common routes you can take:

- If the property will derive its value from some other process in code you would define a **Public** variable in the class module **General Declarations** section and assign this variable a value elsewhere in code. The variable must have the same name as the variable used in the **Property Get** procedure to assign value to the property name.
- Create a method of the object that assigns the property value.

In the case of the read-only property *EmployeeID* (which uses the working local variable named *dblEmpID*) we will create a method named *AssignID*. The method will call a function of the class module that generates a unique serialized number. The procedure for assigning this value is discussed in the next section, which deals with the creation of object methods.

## How to Create a Method for a Class

Methods resolve to standard sub, or (less frequently) function procedures. As the name implies, a method conducts some operation on a member of the class and generally is not expected to return a value as a result. Methods may accept arguments to assist in controlling how to proceed.

As we have been creating a class named *NewEmployee* which contains two fully read/writable properties and a single read-only property (*EmployeeID*). We will discuss the creation of methods by working with two. One to assign an employee ID to the read-only property *EmployeeID* and another method to populate a staff table in the current database with new employee properties.

Because error handling has not yet been discussed note that these methods lack such handlers and would be considered poor programming practice to release such into a production environment. We will include a simple logic block to prevent adding a new record to a staff table if any of the three properties is missing.

Step 1.     Follow Step 1 from the procedure *How to Create a Property of a Class* to ensure that you are not presently within a code block.

Step 2.     Type the term Sub followed by the name of your new method. If the method will accept arguments, within parentheses, name the argument and declare its data type as you would when creating a standard sub procedure). Press **Enter** when done. The VBA editor will stub out the procedure by adding the **End Sub** statement.

Step 3.     Within the **Sub..End Sub** statements, complete any code for your method as desired.

In the case where we need to populate the *EmployeeID* property, we will use a custom function, located within a the class module named *SerialID()*. The function would appear as follows and simply assigns a unique number (the number of seconds transpired from 1 January 1900 to the current time): (Note that the function is **Private**. It should not be exposed as a member of the *NewEmployee* class to code beyond the class module.)

```
Private Function SerialID() As Double
    SerialID = DateDiff("s", #1/1/1900#, Now())
End Function
```

A **Method** named **AssignID** which references this function and populates a variable named *dblEmpID* would appear in the class module as follows:

```
Public Sub AssignID()
    dblEmpID = SerialID
End Sub
```

It is important to note that the variable *dblEmpID* is the **Private** variable created within the class module's **General Declarations** section. It is also referenced as being the variable used to assign a value to the *EmployeeID* property in the **Property Get** statement created a few pages back.

To complete this introductory discussion on user-created objects, we will establish one more method, *CreateEmployee*. This method will generate a SQL statement to insert values into three fields in a table named tblStaffInfo_Class. The **DoCmd** object has a method, **RunSQL** that we can utilize to run our SQL statement and thus populate this table. One point—when you use the **DoCmd** object to manipulate table data, Access will still prompt you when you modify table data even though the table is being manipulated in code. To prevent such messages from appearing when this method is run, we also include paired **DoCmd.SetWarnings** methods to first turn off, and then restore system messages. Access will not conduct such warnings when table data are manipulated using DAO or ADO.

The code for the completed *CreateEmployee* method would appear as following within the class module:

```
Public Sub CreateEmployee()

    Dim strSQL As String
    If Me.EmployeeID = 0 Or Me.LastName = "" _
        Or Me.FirstName = "" Then
        MsgBox "Failed to create employee - data missing"
        Exit Sub
    End If

    strSQL = "INSERT INTO tblStaffInfo_Class (ID, FirstName,
      LastName) "VALUES (" & Me.EmployeeID & ", '" &
      Me.FirstName & "','" & Me.LastName & "');"

    DoCmd.SetWarnings False
    DoCmd.RunSQL strSQL
    DoCmd.SetWarnings True

End Sub
```

The code includes use of the **Me** keyword. Here, like using it with form or report coding, it refers to the current object.

## Creating an Object from a User Defined Class

We're now ready to create an object based on the *NewEmployee* class. You create such an object in a standard code module, or from the code module of a form or report. The process of creating an object from a class is called *instantiation*. The syntax is the same whether you are creating a new object from a built-in class in Access, or from a user-defined object. Instantiation is a two step process. You first create a variable that will become an object of the desired class. What distinguishes this act of creation however is the data type—you refer to a class rather than a standard variable data type. For example, the following code fragment creates a new object variable which references a user-defined class named *NewEmployee*.

```
Dim empNewStaff As NewEmployee
```

When you create code similar to that above, the VBA editor will display the same **Auto List Members** as you encounter when you declare a variable of a standard data type. This is a useful feature as the editor basically lists *all* objects (including any user-defined classes) that you can instantiate.

The second step is again similar to working with variables. You assign the object variable some value. The difference here is the required **Set** keyword that is part of the assignment. **Set** is *always* used when initializing an object variable. Also required for user-defined classes is the **New** keyword.

```
Set empNewStaff = New NewEmployee
```

To repeat the code example this section began with, the following code (based on the properties and methods created in previous examples for the *NewEmployee* class) would create a new employee, assign a unique ID, and populate a staff table:

```
Dim emp As NewEmployee
Set emp = New NewEmployee
emp.FirstName = "Tonya"
emp.LastName = "Johnson"
emp.AssignID
emp.CreateEmployee
```

 **New** specifies that you intend on creating a new instance of an object and not just a reference to an existing object. Although required for user-defined classes, its use is option for built-in classes as we will see shortly.

# Access Objects

Now that we have some understanding of how classes, objects, and their properties and methods are created, it is time to delve more into the objects which make up Microsoft Access. As mentioned earlier, Access objects fall into two distinct categories, the first consists of the Access application itself, and includes the forms, reports, macros, modules, and controls associated with forms and reports. The second group consists of the data objects—these are independent of the Access object model—they make up the tables, queries, relational joins, and all contained data within a database application. The second group of objects will be discussed more fully in Chapter 10.

## The Object Model is Hierarchical

One point of difference between user-defined classes and those classes and their objects which are native to Microsoft Access is the hierarchical nature of the latter group (you can create such hierarchical user-defined objects but that is beyond the subject of this book). Like a long family line, most objects in Access are members of a *collection* , and some objects, especially controls on forms and reports, are *children* of a *parent*—the latter being the form or report that contains the controls. Collections are generally named after the objects they contain but use the plural form, so there is a **Forms** collection that references all open **Form** objects and a **Reports** collect that does the same for **Report** objects. Controls are a special case. There isn't a **Command Buttons** collection—rather, the command button is a **Control** and the containing collection is named **Controls**.

When referencing objects following the hierarchical model, you use the dot notation ( . ) to separate one object from another or to separate an object from a property or method. When referencing a member of a collection, some schemes will require you to use the exclamation mark ( ! ), also known as the *bang operator* , to denote the collection from a member thereof. For example, if you need to read the *caption* property of an open form named *frmProjects* you can employ several schemes. The following examples begin with the most formal and step toward the more informal:

```
Application.Forms![frmProjects].Caption = "Menu"
Forms![frmProjects].Caption= "Menu"
Forms.Item("frmProjects").Caption= "Menu"
Forms("frmProjects").Caption= "Menu"
Me.Caption= "Menu"
```

The first example is the most formal because it fully qualifies the object path by recognizing that the **Application** object (Access itself) contains a property (**Forms**) which serves as a collection of all open forms. The bang operator ( ! ) references a specific form, *frmProjects* and the dot then references the **Caption** property of the form. The second example acknowledges that within the **Application** object, it really isn't necessary to reference anything but the **Forms** collection, hence the shorter syntax. Lastly, the third and fourth examples show the difference between usage of the bang operator vs. the dot when working with members of a collection. In the third example we lose the bang operator since we're not implicitly referring to a member of the **Forms** collection—rather, we're using the **Item** property of the collection and referencing the name of the collection (we could also pass an integer but only if we knew how many forms are open and in particular the ordinal number of the form we are interested in—since this can change in real time, referring to items in a collection by their ordinal number is *never* a good idea). In the forth example you may be wondering why the syntax between it and the second example are dissimilar. The reason is that since we are passing the name of the form as a quote-delimited string *within* parenthesis, we are actually implicitly referring to the **Item** property even thought is isn't mentioned. For most objects, Access and VBA recognize a *default* property which can be implicitly referenced. Good programming practice should deter one from using this type of approach for two reasons. First, Microsoft may at some point remove such implied references to default properties (they have been threatening so in VBA for years!). Second, use of such implied references makes reading the code a bit less clear. Choosing the second or third syntax is far more safe both in terms of future portability and readability.

The last example is also the least formal, and would only work for code running under the a currently open form.

 The use of square brackets around an object name in the previous examples is an option. It is *mandatory* for objects with a space in their name.

## There are Built-in Short Cuts to the Hierarchical Model

Nearly every member of the Microsoft Office Suite has built-in shortcuts to make referencing an object easier and Access is no exception. In the previous code example you have seen that although the **Forms** collection is a child of the **Application** object, within the context of the current database the **Application** object is implied. Beyond some objects being implied, VBA has several objects that make referencing easier. The following table lists the most common shortcuts.

| Shortcut | Description |
|---|---|
| **CurrentProject** | References the currently-opened database file within the **Application** object. This object provides access to certain unique collections, including **AllForms** and **AllReports** (which, unlike the **Forms** and **Reports** collection, tracks *all* forms or reports, whether they are open or not. |
| | Example: **CurrentProject.AllForms.Count** returns the total number of forms in the current database. |
| **CurrentData** | Similar to **CurrentProject** but provides access to collections such as **AllTables** and **AllQueries** |
| | Example: **CurrentData.AllTables.Count** returns the total number of tables in the current database. |
| **Screen** | This object references the current form (**ActiveForm**), report (**ActiveReport**), or the control that currently has the focus (**ActiveControl**). |
| | Example: **Screen.ActiveForm.Name** names the form open and with focus. |
| | Example: **Screen.ActiveControl.Parent.Name** names the form containing the control with the current focus. |
| **Me** | References the current form, report, or user-defined object (only from within the defining class module). |
| | Example: Me.Caption = "Main Menu" sets the caption of the form running this code. |
| | Example: Me.cmdCloseForm.SetFocus sets the focus on a command button named *cmdCloseForm* located on the current form. |

## Working with Collections

The purpose of a collection is to keep track of its members. Most collections have several properties in common, notably **Item** and **Count**. Other common properties include **Parent** and **Application**.

The **Count** property of a collection returns the number of valid members. In a database application that contains 26 forms with only 2 of them currently open, the following code would verify that present state:

```
Debug.Print CurrentProject.AllForms.Count   'returns 26
Debug.Print Forms.Count   'returns 2
```

The **Item** property returns a specific member of the collection. You can reference a member in two ways, by ordinal number (beginning with zero) or by the name of the member. The latter is always the safest route since at run time you may have no idea which index number has been assigned to which member. As mentioned earlier, **Index** is an implied property, so the following statements are syntactically similar. Again, note the use of the bang operator ( ! ) to reference a named member of a collection vs. the dot operator ( . ) when referencing the **Index** property of the collection. (It is assumed **Debug.Print** precedes each statement in order to return results.)

```
CurrentProject.AllForms.Item(3).Name    'returns frmMainMenu
CurrentProject.AllForms![frmMainMenu].Name    'returns
      frmMainMenu

'Next example assumes 18 controls on the only open form,
      frmProjects
Forms.Item(0).Controls.Count    'returns 18
Forms![frmProjects].Controls.Count    'returns 18
'You can cascade the references to collections - here we print
      the name of the 7th control on the form named
      frmProjects.
Forms!frmProjects.Controls.Item(6).Name    'returns
      lblProjectManager
Forms!frmProjects.Controls![lblProjectManager].Caption
      'returns Project Manager
```

## Cycling Through a Collection

VBA provides a looping structure (introduced in Chapter 4) which specifically manages cycling through members of a collection. In this example, a command button named *cmdCountControls* is placed on a form. The code, located in the button's Click event will print the **ControlType** and **Name** for every control on the form:

```
Private Sub cmdCountControls_Click()
    Dim ctrl As Control
    For Each ctrl In Me.Controls
        Debug.Print ctrl.ControlType, ctrl.Name
    Next
End Sub
```

The **ControlType** property returns an integer and not a human-readable name for a control type. On-line help lists the intrinsic constants and you can use the **Immediate Window** to convert these to their integer counterparts. For example, **Print acCommandButton** will return 104 while **Print acLabel** returns 100.

The example below will cycle through all forms in the **AllForms** collection, print the form name and indicate whether the form is currently open or not:

```
Private Sub Allforms_example()
    Dim frm As AccessObject
        For Each frm In CurrentProject.AllForms
        Debug.Print frm.Name, frm.IsLoaded
    Next
End Sub
```

The observant reader may ask why *frm* in the previous code example is an **AccessObject** rather than a form. The answer is that the **AllForms** collection doesn't manage forms, it manages information about the forms in the **CurrentProject**. A review of on-line help for the **AllForms** collection indicates that it returns **AccessObjects** so your object variable must be of the correct object type. The **Forms** collection does manage **Form** objects, but only for forms presently open. The next code example would print out the name of each open form in the **CurrentProject**:

```
Sub AllOpenForms()
    Dim frm As Form
    For Each frm In Forms
        Debug.Print frm.Name
    Next
End Sub
```

This code uses the **DoCmd** object to force a shutdown of all open reports:

```
Sub CloseAllReports()
    Dim rpt As Report
    For Each rpt In Reports
        DoCmd.Close acReport, rpt.Name, acSaveNo
    Next
End Sub
```

Another useful example of cycling through a collection focuses on the controls on a form. In this example as the code cycles through all controls on a form it tests whether the current control is a label or a text box. If true, the **ForeColor** property which specifies the text color is changed to *Red*.

```
Sub ChangeTextColor()

    Dim ctr As Control
    For Each ctr In Me.Controls
        If ctr.ControlType = acTextBox _
            Or ctr.ControlType = acLabel Then
            ctr.ForeColor = vbRed
        End If
    Next

End Sub
```

## Referencing Multiple Object Methods and Properties

Often you need to work with an object and reference several properties and/or methods. Consider the following code fragment that specifies font attributes for a text box on a form:

```
txtData.Font = "Times New Roman"
txtData.FontSize = 10
txtData.FontWeight = 400
txtData.ForeColor = vbRed
txtData.SetFocus
```

VBA provides a streamlined approach to referencing multiple attributes and methods for an object—**With..End With**. The following code fragment is equivalent to the previous code:

```
With txtData
    .Font = "Times New Roman"
    .FontSize = 10
    .FontWeight = 400
    .ForeColor = vbRed
    .SetFocus
End With
```

The structure always begins with the keyword **With** followed by a reference to the desired object. Within the **With..End With** block you refer to any valid property or method (or collection) of the object using the standard dot notation but without having to type the object name. The block occupies a bit more space but saves on typing and helps to organize your code.

# Getting Information About Objects

Access provides three tools for understanding its built-in objects: On-line help, the **Object Browser**, and **Auto List Members**.

## Using On-Line Help

When using On-line Help, if you suspect you are working with an object or a collection, it is generally more useful to search on a fully-qualified term. For example, in on-line help (accessed via the VBA editor and *not* from the Access interface), searching on the term **Form** returns many pages of search results but the **Form** object isn't at the top of the search results. Whereas searching on the term **Form object** returns that topic at the top of the search results. The same is true for searching on **Reports** versus **Reports Collection**. Once you are within the desired topic, generally a link will appear at the bottom that references the **Members** of the object or collection of interest. The **Members** refers to all of the properties, methods (if applicable), and events (if applicable) recognized by the object or collection.

## Using the Object Browser

The **Object Browser** is a tool used to browse through collections, objects, and members from within the VBA code editor.

Step 1.    From within the VBA editor, on the **Standard Toolbar**, click on **Object Browser** (or from the **View** menu, choose **Object Browser**). The **Object Browser** will appear similar to the following:

| Control | Description |
| --- | --- |
| Library Selector | Lists the currently accessible libraries. If you only need to search for an Access object you can limit the results by selecting **Access** from the list of libraries. |
| Search Box | Enter a search term or use the drop down box to select prior search terms. Once a term has been entered or selected, click on the **Search** button to run your search. |
| Help | For the currently-selected **Class** or **Member**, an on-line help topic will appear, if one is available. Otherwise, the generic on-line help page appears. |
| Search Results | Lists all libraries, classes, and members that contain the search term. |
| Classes | For the currently-selected library in the **Search Results**, lists all classes of that library. |
| Members of | For the currently class, lists all members (properties, methods, and events) of that class. |
| Detail Area | Provides a short summary description of the currently selected class or member. |

Step 2.  If desired, select the library you wish to search. Using the default **<All Libraries>** results in the broadest search.

Step 3.  Enter a search term or choose a prior search using the **Search Box**. Select the **Search** button when done.

Step 4.  Browse through the search results. Note that if you are interested in an object within a specific library, selecting any search result with the desired library will synchronize the **Classes** window and you can select the desired object from this list of classes.

Step 5.  If you need information about the **Members** of the selected class, review that list using the **Members of..** window. Properties are noted with a property window icon, events with a lightning bolt, and methods as a small green moving object.

As an example, to review all members of the **Form** object as it exists in Access, select **Access** from the **Libraries** list, then search on the term **Form**. All search results will only reference the **Access** library, so you can move to the **Classes** window and scroll down until you find the **Form** class. Selecting it will list all members of the **Form** object. To learn about a specific property, event, or method of the **Form** object, choose the desired item from the **Members of** window and either choose the **Help** button or press *F1*.

The **Object Browser** occupies the **Code Window** when open. You must close the **Object Browser** to return to the **Code Window**.

## Using Auto List Members

This feature of the VBA editor was introduced in Chapter 1, but now that objects have been introduced this is a good time to revisit this useful feature of the VBA editor. When you are writing code and the VBA editor understands the context sufficiently **Auto List Members** will appear as you type the name of an object or a collection and complete the name with the dot operator. This is similar to using the **Members of..** window on the **Object Browser** and **Auto List members** will list all properties, events, and methods of that object or collection. The example below shows **Auto List Members** appearing after the **DoCmd** object was referenced in code:

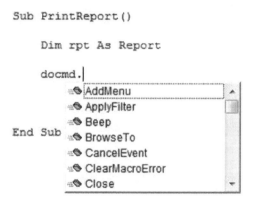

```
Sub PrintReport()

    Dim rpt As Report

    docmd.|
            AddMenu
            ApplyFilter
            Beep
End Sub      BrowseTo
            CancelEvent
            ClearMacroError
            Close
```

This is a powerful way to learn about the properties, methods, and events associated with an object. The icons are the same as for the **Members of..** window in the **Object Browser**. On-line help isn't immediately available via this tool, but selecting a member of the list and then pressing *F1* will open help to that member.

# Chapter 7 | User Interface Objects

In an Access database application, Forms are the most common and useful interface objects. Users interact with forms to conduct data entry and edit operations, review summary information, and open other forms or reports. Reports present table data and are frequently used to create sophisticated grouping and summaries of data. Using forms and reports in this manner will be discussed in the next chapter. Here, we will instead mention three useful objects that assist in obtaining information from the end user during run time. Two of these objects, the **MsgBox** (message box) and **InputBox** are native to Microsoft Access. The third, **FileDialog** is owned by Microsoft Office. All three look like regular Windows system objects your end users are familiar with and are important tools for obtaining information.

## Working with the MsgBox Object

The Message Box is used in one of two modes. As a **Statement** the message box simply presents information to your user. In this mode you code the message box so it only presents a single command button with an *OK* caption. The other mode is as a **Function**, and like all functions, returns a value. In the case of a message box, the value represents which button on the dialog box the user selected.

Message boxes are *modal* dialog boxes, meaning that when present, no other window within Access can gain the focus. The user must address the message box by selecting one of its command buttons or by closing the dialog window.

Message boxes accept 5 arguments as detailed in the following table.

# MsgBox Arguments

| Argument | Description |
| --- | --- |
| **Prompt** | A string value that will appear as the message on the message box. It should not exceed 1024 characters. If you wish to include line breaks you can include the carriage return, Chr(13), a line feed, Chr(10), or a carriage return-line feed-combination. The intrinsic constants for these special characters are vbCR, vbLF, and vbCRLF, respectively. This is the only required argument. |
| **Buttons** | A numeric value that represents the type of button(s) displayed, the type of icon, the default button, presence of a **Help** button, text alignment, and modality of the message box. See the next table for details.<br><br>The **Buttons** argument accepts integer values but there is a strong utility in using intrinsic constants for readability and future maintenance on your code. When you need a specific set of buttons *and* a message icon you *add* the values together. Example: vbYesNo + vbQuestion. If not specified, the default is vbOKOnly. |
| **Title** | An optional string that will appear on the message box title bar. If omitted, *Microsoft Access* will appear as the default title. |
| **HelpFile** | A fully-qualified path and filename to a *hlp* or *chm* file. If this value is present then the **Context** argument *must* appear. |
| **Context** | An integer that references the *Help ID* from the **HelpFile**. If not known, pass a zero which will open the help file title page. |

The intrinsic constants for the **Button** argument are outlined in the following table.

| Constant | Description |
|---|---|
| **vbOkOnly, vbOkCancel, vbAbortRetryIgnore, vbYesNoCancel, vbYesNo, vbRetryCancel, vbMsgBoxHelpButton** | These are the 6 available button combinations for the Message Box, plus an additional argument to present a **Help** button. |
| **vbCritical, vbQuestion, vbExclamation, vbInformation** | There are 4 message box icons. You can only format for one icon. If no icon constants are present the message box will only display the prompt text along with any specified buttons. |
| **vbDefaultButton1, vbDefaultButton2, vbDefaultButton3, vbDefaultButton4** | Sets which button is the default (pressing **Return** will fire the button). vbDefaultButton4 is only available if you choose a 3-button style *plus* vbMsgBoxHelpButton. |
| **vbApplicationModal, vbSystemModal, VbMsgBoxSetForeground** | The first constant is the default. No other Access window can gain the focus until the message box is closed. The second constant forces *all* applications to be suspended until the message box is closed. The third argument forces the **MsgBox** to keep above all other windows. |
| **vbMsgBoxRight, vbMsgBoxRltReading** | First constant right-aligns the text associated with **Prompt**, the second argument is used for right-to-left text streaming (Hebrew and Arabic languages only). |

If you use **MsgBox** as a function, it returns an integer value representing the button that was selected by the user. The following table lists the constants and their integer value. The last code example in this section shows the use of a **Select Case** statement to react to a user's choice.

| Constant | Value |
|---|---|
| **vbOk** | 1 |
| **vbCancel** | 2 |
| **vbAbort** | 3 |
| **vbRetry** | 4 |
| **vbIgnore** | 5 |
| **vbYes** | 6 |
| **vbNo** | 7 |

## MsgBox as a Statement

To use the **MsgBox** as a statement, you must provide a prompt and leave the default button type as vbOK. You may include other **Buttons** values such as an icon or to present a **Help** button but because as a statement the **MsgBox** will not return information concerning which button has been selected. It is very poor programming practice to include other button types as they will have no effect. The following code would result in a message box appearing as:

```
MsgBox "The database was backed up successfully",
    vbInformation
```

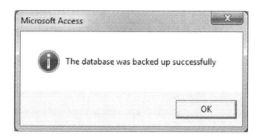

## MsgBox as a Function

When you use **MsgBox** as a function there are two additional points. First, you must assign a variable of the **Integer** data type that will accept the return value from the function. The return value corresponds to an intrinsic constant that identifies which button the user selected. Second, the argument list *must* be enclosed in parentheses—like all function argument lists.

The following code uses a **MsgBox** as a function:

```
intReply = MsgBox("Are you sure you want to delete this
    record", vbYesNo + vbQuestion)
```

If the user selects the **Yes** button the **MsgBox** function returns the intrinsic constant *vbYes*, otherwise it returns *vbNo*. A **Select Case** logic block is typically used to control program flow at this point as in the following code fragment:

```
Dim intReply As Integer
Dim strQuestion As String

strQuestion = "Are you sure you wish to delete this record?"

intReply = MsgBox(strQuestion, vbYesNo + vbQuestion)

Select Case intReply
    Case vbYes
        'code to delete the record goes here
    Case vbNo
        'any code to save the record goes here, otherwise
      ignore vbNo and exit the sub
End Select
```

# Working with the InputBox Object

The **InputBox** displays a prompt and a text box and is used to receive text input from the user. In this regard it is different from a **MsgBox**, which only returns a constant indicating which button the user selected. Input boxes are modal as well. If the user does not enter text into the **InputBox** and there is no defined default text, the function will return a *zero length string*. This function accepts up to 7 arguments as detailed in the following table.

# InputBox Arguments

| Argument | Description |
| --- | --- |
| **Prompt** | A string value that will appear as the message on the input box. It should not exceed 1024 characters. If you wish to include line breaks you can include the carriage return, Chr(13), a line feed, Chr(10), or a carriage return-line feed-combination. The intrinsic constants for these special characters are vbCR, vbLF, and vbCRLF, respectively. This is the only required argument. |
| **Title** | An optional string that will appear on the input box title bar. If omitted, *Microsoft Access* will appear as the default title. |
| **Default** | An optional string to appear in the text area of the input box. If the user chooses **Cancel** this value is returned by the **InputBox** function. |
| **XPos** | An optional numeric value that controls, in *Twips* the left-to-right positioning of the input box as measured from the left screen margin. The input box is centered left-to-right if this argument is not specified. |
| **YPos** | Similar to **XPos** except this argument specifies top-to-bottom alignment, measured from the screen top. |
| **HelpFile** | A fully-qualified path and filename to a *hlp* or *chm* file. If this value is present then the **Context** argument *must* appear. |
| **Context** | An integer that references the *Help ID* from the **HelpFile**. If not known, pass a zero which will open the help file title page. |

## Processing the InputBox Return Value

Because **InputBox** is a function, your code must accept the returned string value and should react to it. Although error handling will be addressed in greater detail in Chapter 9, input boxes are a good example of the disconnect that can occur between the programmer's ideal world and the real world of the end user. A good example of this would be to begin with the following input box:

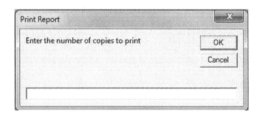

You are expecting the end user to enter a numeric value (we'll talk about type conversion next) and the end user instead types *fore*. It can be a bit of a surprise when the input isn't what you expect, especially when a user can't even spell correctly!

Working with input boxes is a good lesson in having to consider the difference between expected input and actual input. The following code fragment would be helpful in keeping end users under control:

```vba
Sub PrintReport()
Dim strReply As String

strReply = InputBox("Enter the number of copies to print",
    "Print Report")

If Not IsNumeric(strReply) Then
    MsgBox "Please enter a number!"
    Exit Sub
Else
    If strReply < 1 Then
        MsgBox "Cannot print zero or fewer copies"
        Exit Sub
    ElseIf strReply > 10 Then
        Dim intReply As Integer
        Dim strText As String
        strText = "You sure you want to print " & strReply & "
        copies?"
        intReply = MsgBox(strText, vbYesNo, "Verify Print
        Job")
            If intReply = vbNo Then Exit Sub
    End If
End If
    'start printing!
    Dim intCounter As Integer
    For intCounter = 1 To strReply
        DoCmd.OpenReport rptReport, acViewReport
    Next intCounter
End Sub
```

The above code example illustrates defensive coding. There are several places in the code that serve as a reality check, the first being the **If** block that tests whether the return variable, *strReply* is a number or not. If it isn't, a message is formatted and code execution leaves the sub procedure. A second reality check tests to make sure the number is greater than zero, and again, if this condition isn't met a message is formatted and program flow leaves the procedure. Lastly, an optional test reacts to numbers greater than 10. If the user specifies 11 or more copies they are asked whether they are sure about printing this number of copies. If not, code execution leaves the procedure. If so, the procedure flows normally toward the logic block where **DoCmd.OpenReport** is called.

You may think it curious that a variable of the String data type is working for numeric operations such as **If strReply < 1 Then..** VBA is pretty good at simple coercion of data when working between string , date/time, and numeric values, in part because the numerals 0-9 are also text values that sort in the same order as integer values and because dates generally contain string characters. There are times however, when you may need to force a conversion between data types, especially when working with the **InputBox** function. If you need to force a data type conversion, use one of the type conversion functions.

 There are several type conversion functions that manage changing data from one data type to another. From the VBA editor, open on-line help and search on the phrase *type conversion functions*.

# Working with the File Dialog

The third user interface object isn't a member of VBA—instead this object is a member of the Microsoft Office Suite. VBA can easily handle working with objects from other applications as long as you include a reference to the desired object library (this is discussed in more detail in Chapter 12). If you fail to create such a reference the VBA editor will be unable to display items such as **Auto List Members** since it will be unaware of the object and its associated members. Additionally, a compile time error will be generated when you run your code.

## How to Add a Library Reference

The **FileDialog** object is a member of the Microsoft Office Suite. The library for objects associated with this application is named **Microsoft Office *versionNumber* Object Library**. If you are working on a computer with several versions of the office suite you should choose the object library with the highest version number.

Step 1.    From within the VBA code editor, select the **Tools** menu, then choose **References...** The **References** dialog will appear similar to the following:

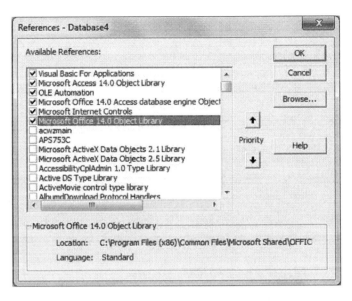

Step 2.    If the desired library is not visible, scroll through the list in the **Available References** area. Once located, place a check to the left of the library name.

Step 3.    Choose **OK** to add the reference.

You would uncheck a library to remove it from your project. To ensure such an action doesn't leave unreferenced objects choose the **Debug** menu then select **Compile**. If no errors are generated your code is free of unreferenced objects.

## About the FileDialog Object

The **FileDialog** object is essentially a file browser. It does not open the file or files that are selected. Rather, it simply returns the full drive/path/filename specification for the selected file or files. If no files are selected the **Show** property returns *False*.

The following table outlines the more common methods and properties of this object:

| Member | Description |
| --- | --- |
| AllowMultiselect | Permits selection of two or more files (property). |
| Filters | A collection of file type filters. The **Clear** method removes all filters while the **Add** method adds a new filter. If using **Add** you must specify two arguments, a string-delimited filter name and a string-delimited filter expression. Example: **.Filters.Add "text file", "*.txt"** (collection/property). |
| InitialFileName | A property that specifies the drive, folder, and/or file to list when the dialog box opens. Example: **.InitialFileName="C:\"** would open to display the root of the C: drive. |
| InitialView | Sets the file view type for the dialog box. The next table lists the constants for this property. |
| SelectedItems | Represents a collection of the one or more files which have been selected. You either enumerate this collection or reference individual files. For example if only one file is selected you can access it by using **SelectedItems.Item(1)** (collection/property). |
| Show | A method that opens the **FileDialog**. It returns *True* if at least one file was selected. If the user presses **Cancel**, this method returns *False*. |
| | When this method is called *all* execution stops and the **FileDialog** becomes a *modal* dialog. The user must select a file or press **Cancel** to close the dialog. Once closed your code continues execution on the next line following the call to the **Show** method. |
| Title | A property that sets the caption for the **FileDialog**. |

# InitialView Constants

| Constant | Description |
| --- | --- |
| msoFileDialogViewDetails | Files displayed in a list with detail information. |
| msoFileDialogViewLargeIcons | Files displayed as large icons. |
| msoFileDialogViewList | Files displayed in a list without details. |
| msoFileDialogViewSmallIcons | Files displayed as small icons. |
| msoFileDialogViewThumbnail | Files displayed as thumbnails. |
| msoFileDialogViewPreview | Files displayed in a list with a preview pane showing the selected file. |
| msoFileDialogViewProperties | Files displayed in a list with a pane showing the selected file's properties. |
| msoFileDialogViewTiles | Files displayed as tiled icons. |
| msoFileDialogViewWebView | Files displayed in Web view. |

The following code example illustrates how to use the **FileDialog** object. It assumes that there is a text box named *txtFileName* that will display the fully-qualified file selected using the **FileDialog**. The **FileDialog** is opened from within the Click event for a command button on a form.

```
Private Sub cmdOpenFile_Click()

    ' Requires reference to Microsoft Office 11.0 Object
        Library.
    Dim fd As Office.FileDialog
    Dim varFileRef As Variant

    ' Clear listbox contents on the form.
    Me.txtFileText.Value = ""
    Me.txtFileName.Value = ""

    ' Set up the File Dialog.
    Set fd = Application.FileDialog(msoFileDialogFilePicker)

    With fd
        .Title = "Please select a text file to read"
        ' Clear out the current filters, and add custom.
        .Filters.Clear
        .Filters.Add "text file", "*.txt"
        .Filters.Add "web page", "*.html"
        .Filters.Add "rich text", "*.rtf"
        ' Show the dialog box. If the .Show method returns
        ' True, the user picked at least one file. If the
        ' .Show method returns False, the user Cancelled.
        If .Show = True Then
            If .SelectedItems.Item(1) <> "" Then
                Me.txtFileName.Value = .SelectedItems.Item(1)
        Else
                MsgBox "You didn't select a valid file."
                Exit Sub
            End If
        Else
            MsgBox "The operation was cancelled."
        End If
    End With

End Sub
```

To process multiple file selection you need to first set the **AllowMultiSelect** property to true, then enumerate through the collection of selected files as in this code fragment:

```
Dim fd As Office.FileDialog
Dim varFileRef As Variant
Set fd = Application.FileDialog(msoFileDialogFilePicker)
Fd.AllowMultiSelect = True
With Fd
    .Filters.Clear
    .Filters.Add "All Files", "*.*"
    If .Show = True Then
        For Each varFileRef in .SelectedItems
            Debug.Print varFileRef
        Next
    End if
End With
```

As outlined in the code examples above, calling the **Show** method of the **FileDialog** object forces the object to appear to the user. It is a modal dialog box and the user must either select a file (or files if so permitted) or choose **Cancel** or close the dialog box without making a selection. Any code beyond the call to the **Show** method does not run until the **Open** or **Cancel** buttons are selected. An example of such a FileDialog object during run time is illustrated below.

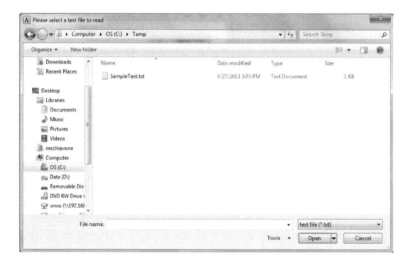

# Chapter 8 | Form and Report Programming

Forms and Reports serve as the starting point for nearly all VBA code associated with an application. Forms and Reports are complex objects. They serve as containers for entire collections of controls (including the **Detail** area and various **Header** and **Footer** objects). As data-bound objects they are capable of responding to numerous events related to their role as data presentation or data editing objects. They may also host data-bound controls which themselves respond to a myriad of data-aware and user-aware events.

 This Chapter assumes a good working knowledge of forms and reports. There is a book in this series, *Building Forms and Reports using Microsoft Access 2010* that presents the creation of forms and reports in great detail.

## Form and Report Events

Events were introduced in Chapter 3 from a general perspective. Here we will discuss the most commonly used events for both Forms and Reports. Some events pertain to a form or report regardless of whether it is bound to a data source. Other events only have context when working with bound objects. The following table highlights the most important events for these objects.

| Event | Object | Description |
|---|---|---|
| Activate / Deactivate | Form / Report | **Activate** is triggered when a form or a report receives focus *and becomes the active window*. **Deactivate** fires when the focus is moved to another window. |
| Before/After Del Confirm | Form | **BeforeDelConfirm** triggers once one or more records have been deleted (placed in the delete buffer) but *before* a message box asking to confirm the delete operation is presented. **AfterDelConfirm** is triggered once the user confirms the delete operation or cancels the deletion of records. |
| Before/After Insert | Form / bound form controls | **BeforeInsert** fires after the first character change to a control on a form *for a new record*. It accepts an argument, **Cancel** which if set to *True* cancels the event. **AfterInsert** is triggered after the record has been created. It is a good place to code events which may requery the form or other forms that need to know about the newly added record. |
| Before/After Update | Form / bound form controls | **BeforeUpdate** occurs when data has been changed but *before* the change is committed to the record source. It accepts an argument, *Cancel*, that if set to *True* will cancel the event (you would still need to call the **Undo** method for the form or control to undo any edits). **AfterUpdate** occurs once the change is committed to the record source. |
| Current | Form | Is evoked when a form opens and displays the first record and again each time the user steps to another record, or if the form is requeried. Occurs after **Open**, **Load**, **Resize**, and **Activate**. Technically this event is recognized by reports but has little programming utility for that object. |
| Delete | Form | Fires when the user moves to delete a record but before the deletion. The argument **Cancel**, if set to *True* cancels the deletion. This is an excellent event for prompting the user if they are certain they wish to delete a record. |
| Dirty | Form | Is triggered after a single character change to any bound control on the form. The argument **Cancel**, if set to *True* will cancel the change. Once triggered, the **Dirty** property of the form is set to *True* and remains in this state until the current record is saved. Technically this event is recognized by reports but is nonsensical in that context. |
| Enter/Exit | Some bound form controls | **Enter** fires when the focus enters a control (such as a text box, option group, combo box or subform) but before the **GotFocus** event is triggered. **Exit** triggers before a control fires its **LostFocus** event. |
| Format | Report sections | This event is triggered for report sections (headers and footers) as well as the **Detail** section when Access determines which data will appear in the section but before it is formatted for preview or printing. |

| Event | Object | Description |
|---|---|---|
| Got/Lost Focus | Form Controls | **GotFocus** fires every time the focus (either via mouse or keyboard) enters a control. It is only applicable to the **Form** object if the form lacks controls or if all controls have been disabled. **LostFocus** is triggered when the focus leaves a control. **GotFocus** fires after **Enter**. **LostFocus** fires after **Exit**. |
| Load, Unload | Form / Report | **Load** triggers when a form or report is open *and* the records are displayed. It fires after **Open** but before **Resize**, **Activate**, and **Current**. **Unload** is triggered after a form or report is closed but *before* it is removed from the screen. **Unload** is triggered before **Deactivate** and **Close**. |
| NoData | Report | This event is triggered when a report has been formatted and the record source is empty. The event fires before the report is displayed in **Report** or **Print Preview** view. |
| Page | Report | Fires when a page has been formatted but before it is printed or appears in **Print Preview**. |
| Print | Report sections | This event fires once a section has been formatted for printing but before it is previewed or actually printed. |
| Open, Close | Form / Report | **Open** fires when the form or report is being opened but before any data are displayed. The Open event accepts an argument, *Cancel*, and if *True* cancels opening for form or report. **Close** fires when the form or report is closed and removed from the screen. |

# Referencing Other Forms and Reports

The object model for forms and reports becomes apparent when you need to refer to a form or report (or one of the embedded controls) from another form, report, or module. These inter-object calls always require you to formally step through the object model. Such calls begin by referring to either the **Forms** or the **Reports** collection, which tracks all open forms and reports, respectively. Recall from Chapters 5 and 6 that you cannot refer to an object on a closed form or report (from the perspective of *scope* and *lifetime* a closed form or report doesn't exist), and that the **AllForms** and **AllReports** collections only track the names of all forms and reports in a database. When a form or report is closed both Access and VBA consider it to be unavailable for referencing except as a named item in the **AllForms** and **AllReports** collections.

## Referring to Controls on Another Form or Report

The following code fragments illustrate how to refer to another form, report, or a control on a form or report.

To refer to a control (here named *txtSearchLastName*) located on a form named *frmSearch*:

```
Forms!frmSearch.txtSearchLastName        'or..
Forms!frmSearch.Controls!txtSearchLastName    'or..
Forms(frmSearch).txtSearchLastName    'or..
Forms(frmSearch).Controls!txtSearchLastName    'or
Forms(frmSearch).Controls(txtSearchLastName)
```

 Recall from the discussion about bang syntax (on page 106) that one uses the exclamation mark to separate an object from its collection. The exclamation mark isn't required in the schemes above where instead the object is named (within parenthesis) as a member of that collection.

The **Value** property of the text box is the default property and is assumed if no property is mentioned. For any other property you must provide the property name. For example, to reference the **Caption** property of an open form named *frmMainMenu*:

```
Forms!frmMainMenu.Caption    'or
Forms(frmMainMenu).Caption
```

The same general syntax works for open reports as well.

To reference a control on a subform or a subreport you must drill down deeper into the object model. For a Form named *frmProjects* which contains a subform named *sbfProjectStaffing* that contains a bound text box named *txtDepartment*, the syntax becomes:

```
Forms!frmProjects.sbjProjectStaffing.Form.txtDepartment
```

Referring to an open report is a bit different in that VBA only fully "sees" the open report when displayed in **Report View**. Once the report has been opened in **Print Preview** you cannot access many properties of a subreport, although the report itself is still accessible via VBA. The following code refers to a bound text box named *Budget* located on a subreport named *sbfProjectStaffing* on a report named *rptBudgetInfo*:

```
Reports.rptBudgetInfo.sbfProjectStaffing.Controls.Budget
```

Any of the variations between use of the bang operator and dot notation illustrated above for forms works identically when referencing reports and their objects.

# Examples of Form and Report Programming

We present a few examples here that illustrate the power of using VBA behind a form or a report. In each case, VBA brings functionality to the application which otherwise would not be possible.

## Emulating a Bound Image Control

The **Image** control is an unbound control that is normally used to present a static image such as a corporate logo on a form or report. Using a **Bound Object Frame** to display graphic information such as staff pictures has its drawbacks, as storing binary data such as images within the database results in greatly increased database file sizes.

When you need to display graphic information associated with database records, the alternative is to store the graphic file name (and path if necessary) as text data. An **Image** control can be made to emulate being a bound control with a little bit of VBA code behind the Form's **Current** event.

In this example, a table that stores information about staff has been modified to also include a text field that references the name of an image file for each staff member. The images themselves are located outside of the database but in a folder accessible to the database application (in this case in a folder named *Graphics* off the root directory that the database is stored in).

An image control (here named *imgStaffImage* is placed on the form. We use the form's **Current** event as it fires upon first connection to the form's record source and subsequently upon movement to a record. The code appears as:

```
Private Sub Form_Current()
    If Not IsNull(Me.StaffImage) Then
        Me.imgStaffImage.Picture = CurrentProject.Path & _
            "\Graphics\" & Me.StaffImage
        Me.imgStaffImage.Requery
    Else  'clear the image control if no picture exists
        Me.imgStaffImage.Picture = ""
        Me.imgStaffImage.Requery
    End If
End Sub
```

An example of a form using this technique appears below.

This technique can be applied to any control that displays data. The **Current** event is an excellent location for code that must be sensitive to the current record on a bound form.

## Creating a Search Form

Using VBA you can manipulate a form's **Record Source** property dynamically. In this example, a form is set to display *Continuous records* (the **Default View** property of the form). For simplicity, only 4 of the bound fields are included in the **Detail** area. The Form's **Header** includes several unbound controls: 2 text boxes to accept search strings for either *LastName* or *Department* (the controls are named *txtLastName* and *txtDepartment*, respectively). Two check boxes (*chkWildcardLastname* and *chkWildcardDepartment*) control whether the *LastName* and *Department* search values must be literal or can be wildcards. The code illustrated below is associated with a command button (*cmdSearch*) and appears in the *Click* event. The form as viewed in **Design View** appears below:

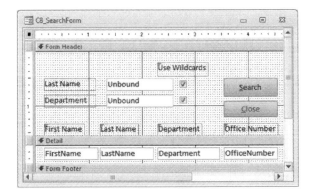

When the form first opens all records from the underlying **Record Source**, *tblStaffInfo* appear in the **Detail** area. If the user enters text in either or both search boxes and selects **Search**, the code is processed. The end goal of the VBA code is the creation of one of the following SQL statements (depending upon the state of the *txtLastName*, *chkWildcardLastName*, *txtDepartment*, and *chkWildcardDepartment* controls:

1. LastName not null, last name wildcard not checked, Department box is null:

SELECT * FROM tblStaffInfo WHERE LastName='*txtLastName*';

2. Same as above except last name wildcard is checked:

SELECT * FROM tblStaffInfo WHERE LastName LIKE '**txtLastname***';

3. The same two states above, except applying to the Department controls:

SELECT * FROM tblStaffInfo WHERE Department ='*txtDepartment*';

SELECT * FROM tblStaffInfo WHERE Department LIKE '**txtDepartment*';

4. No wildcards, both LastName and Department text boxes have values:

SELECT * FROM tblStaffInfo WHERE LastName='*txtLastName*' AND Department='*txtDepartment*';

5. As above but LastName wildcard checked:

SELECT * FROM tblStaffInfo WHERE LastName LIKE '**txtLastName***' AND Department ='*txtDepartment*';

The remaining 3 possible states are permutations on the fifth example, using the LIKE operator for the Department criteria only or for both the LastName and Department criteria. The final state occurs if no control is checked or contains a search value. In this case all records are returned:

SELECT * FROM tblStaffInfo;

These various states are derived using the following VBA code:

```vba
Private Sub cmdSearch_Click()
  Dim strSQLName As String
  Dim strSQLDept As String
  Dim strSQL     As String
'build the initial search strings and enclose
'in wildcard characters if requested
  If Not IsNull(txtLastName.Value) Then
    If chkWildcardLastName.Value = True Then
      strSQLName = "[LastName] LIKE '*" & _
      txtLastName.Value & "*'"
    Else
      strSQLName = "[LastName]='" & _
      txtLastName.Value & "'"
    End If
  End If
  If Not IsNull(txtDepartment.Value) Then
    If chkWildcardDepartment.Value = True Then
      strSQLDept = "[Department] LIKE '*" & _
      txtDepartment.Value & "*'"
    Else
      strSQLDept = "[Department]='" & _
      txtDepartment.Value & "'"
    End If
  End If

'now add the two variables together if both are not empty
  If strSQLName <> "" And strSQLDept <> "" Then
    strSQL = "SELECT * FROM [tblStaffInfo] WHERE " _
    & strSQLName & " AND " & strSQLDept
  ElseIf strSQLName <> "" Then
    strSQL = "SELECT * FROM [tblStaffInfo] WHERE " _
    & strSQLName
  ElseIf strSQLDept <> "" Then
    strSQL = "SELECT * FROM [tblStaffInfo] WHERE " _
    & strSQLDept
  Else
    strSQL = "SELECT * FROM [tblStaffInfo]"
  End If

'Add the terminating semicolon
  strSQL = strSQL & ";"
'Update the form Record Source
  Me.RecordSource = strSQL
  Me.Requery
End Sub
```

The code works toward building a valid SQL SELECT query which bound forms will accept as record sources. The first major logic block builds the criteria part of a WHERE clause searching on *LastName* if the *txtLastName* text box isn't empty. Depending upon the state of the wildcard check box for *LastName*, the code encloses the search term in wildcard characters. The second major logic block conducts the same operation but for the *Department* field. The third logic block merges the WHERE clause criteria using 1 of 4 possible states:

- Both *txtLastName* and *txtDepartment* controls have values. In this case the WHERE clause must include both search terms *ANDed* together.

- Only the *txtLastName* control has data. The WHERE clause will only search the *LastName* field.

- Only the *txtDepartment* control has data. The WHERE clause will only search the *Department* field.

- Neither control has data. There will be no WHERE clause—all records will be returned.

The following illustration shows this form in operation. As an extreme case, both wildcard checkboxes have been selected. The form is displaying results where the letter *e* occurs anywhere in a person's last name AND they work in a department where the department name contains the letter pair *an*.

## Creating a Report Switchboard

It is common in database applications to call reports from a switchboard form. It is also common to configure the report so that its records are filtered based on some setting on a control on the switchboard form. An example below illustrates this point:

The controls on this form have the following attributes:

| Control | Attributes |
| --- | --- |
| Frame | Unbound, contains only 2 radio buttons with captions *Staff Listing* (value=1) and *Department Listing* (value = 2). The checkbox and combo box were simply drawn on top of the frame after it was created. |
| Check Box | Captioned as **All Departments**. Control name is *chkStaffReportAllDepartments,* Default Value property set to *True*. |
| Combo Box | Unbound and named *cboStaffReportDepartments*. The RowSource property is set to the SQL statement SELECT DISTINCT Department FROM tblStaffInfo ORDER BY Department; This creates a unique list of all departments listed in a field named *Department* in a table named *tblStaffInfo*. |
| Command Button | Named *cmdPrint* and captioned *Print*. The bulk of the code is in the *Click* event for this control. |
| Check Box | Named *chkPreview* and captioned *Print Preview*, its Default Value property is set to *True*. |

Code is required in just two locations. The first bit of code is relatively trivial. As the *All Departments* check box is toggled, it alternatively enables or disables the *Departments* combo box.

This serves as a visual reminder to the end user that selecting *All Departments* means you cannot select a department from the combo box. The code, located in the *Click* event for the *chkStaffReportAllDepartments* check box is:

```
If Me.chkStaffReportAllDepartments.Value = True Then
    Me.cboStaffReportDepartments.Enabled = False
Else
    Me.cboStaffReportDepartments.Enabled = True
End If
```

It should be noted that some programmers would have preferred an even shorter (albeit a bit more difficult to read version:

```
Me.cboStaffReportDepartments.Enabled = Not
        me.chkStaffReportAllDepartments.Value
```

The bulk of the code appears in the *Click* event for the *cmdPrint* command button:

```
Private Sub cmdPrint_Click()

'set up the variables needed
Dim strReportName As String
Dim strFilter     As String
Dim intOpenMode   As Integer

'determine how to open the report
If Me.chkPreview.Value = True Then
    intOpenMode = acViewPreview
Else
    intOpenMode = acViewNormal
End If

'determine which report to open
Select Case Me.fraReportType.Value
  Case 1  'staff report
    strReportName = "StaffInfo_Simple"
    'all staff records or filtered?
    If Me.chkStaffReportAllDepartments.Value = True Then
        strFilter = ""
    Else 'filter on department if not null
        If IsNull(Me.cboStaffReportDepartments) Then
            MsgBox "Please select a department"
            Exit Sub
        End If
        'we have a valid dept listed in the combo box
        strFilter = "[Department]='" &_
            Me.cboStaffReportDepartments & "'"
    End If
  Case 2  'department report
    strReportName = "StaffInfo_Grouped"
End Select

'call the OpenReport method and pass variables
DoCmd.OpenReport strReportName, intOpenMode, , strFilter

End Sub
```

## Opening a Report Conditionally

Continuing with the previous code example, you may decide that the report *StaffInfo_Simple* should not open unless the switchboard form (here named *frmSwitchboard* is open. This is a pretty brief bit of code that would be located in the report's **Open** event:

```
If CurrentProject.AllForms("frmSwitchboard").IsLoaded = False
    Then
    Cancel = True
Else 'it is open but may be in design view!
    If Forms("C8_ReportSwitchboard").CurrentView <> 1 Then
        Cancel = True
    End If
End If
```

The previous code fragment is a good example of the machinations programmers sometimes have to run to achieve a simple goal, especially when there are multiple paths to a common goal. In this example we use the **AllForms** collection to first test whether the form is loaded or not. If it is, **AllForms** can't distinguish between open in **Form** or **Design** view so we need to now switch to the **Forms** collection, which can tell you whether a form is open in **Form View** (the **CurrentView** property returns *1* if open in **Form View** and *0* if open in **Design View**. Another approach to this problem would be to test the **Forms** collection and if an error occurs (and is trapped—see Chapter 9) then for form isn't open.

## Creating a Table of Contents for a Report

When generating large reports is may be useful to include a table of contents (TOC). This isn't an intrinsic feature of Microsoft Access but there are ways to achieve a table of contents using VBA. We haven't discussed the Data Access Object (DAO) yet, and we will return to this problem in Chapter 11. Here we will create a table of contents using SQL statements which fire using the **RunSQL** method of the **DoCmd** object.

To create a table of contents for a report:

- The VBA code that will create each TOC entry goes into the **Print** event on a report. Depending upon your focus and the structure of the report, the **Detail** or a group **Header** is a good place to locate the code. For example, if you have a grouped report and want the TOC to list detailed entries the code would go in the **Detail** section's **Print** event. To only focus on major grouping, the code would instead be located in the **Print** event for the desired group **Header**.

- A table must exist that will accept the TOC entries. At a minimum it should contain a text field for the topic and a number field for the page number. Because it is possible to generate duplicate entries (as Access considers how to insert page breaks) this table should not contain a unique index on either field or a primary key made up of the two fields.

- A separate report will be created that will contain the table of contents. It should use a query as its **Record Source** and the query should pull records from the TOC table using a SELECT DISTINCT clause to eliminate duplicate entries.

- For a complete TOC to be generated you must either move to the last page of the primary report while in **Print Preview** view or physically print the entire report. The reason for this is that Access must visit every page on the report in order to make a final decision as to which information goes on which page.

We will omit the creation of the TOC table and TOC report and instead focus on the VBA code. In this example, we are using a grouped report that lists projects by department. The TOC focus will be on the individual departments so code will appear in two places: the **Open** event for the report (to clear the TOC table of any existing data) and the **Print** event for the **Department** group header.

To clear existing results the code would appear as:

```
Private Sub Report_Open(Cancel As Integer)

    'first clear existing TOC
    With DoCmd
        .SetWarnings False
        .RunSQL "DELETE * FROM tblTOC;"
        .SetWarnings True
    End With

End Sub
```

The code that populates the tblTOC table would appear in the **Print** event for the **Department** header:

```
Private Sub GroupHeader0_Print(Cancel As Integer, PrintCount _
        As Integer)

'populate table with new data
With DoCmd
  .SetWarnings False
  .RunSQL "INSERT INTO tblTOC VALUES('" & Me.Department & _
        "'," & Me.Page & ");"
  .SetWarnings True
End With

End Sub
```

Note the inclusion of single quotes around the value *me.Department*. This field in the *tblTOC* table is text and thus must be comma-delimited. The field value for *me.Page* is numeric and does not require delimitation.

***Warning***: Field values that contain apostrophes will not be inserted into the table! If you need to build a TOC with data that contains apostrophes you need to delimit the delimiter. This is done by using double apostrophes ( '') rather than singles. The following code uses the **Replace()** function to achieve this result:

Replace(me.Department, " ' ", " " ")

The spaces within the second and third argument were added for clarity and should not appear unless you intend to replace text containing such spaces.

Once your primary report has been fully previewed or printed, you would call a second report that uses the *tblTOC* as its **Record Source**,  thus creating your table of contents for the primary report.

# Chapter 9 | Error Handling

Errors can appear nearly anywhere in code, and can surface during different times (for example a syntax error arises when you are creating code while a run time error occurs when your code is executing). We will first address the simple ones: the errors that appear during *compile time* and relate generally to syntax errors in your code. The more difficult classes are also addressed. *Logic Errors* may appear as seemingly well-written blocks of code but do not run as expected. *Run Time* errors also occur during program execution and usually can't be predicted, except to the extent that a seasoned developer understands that "anything" can happen. This last class can utilize *Error Trapping*, which will be presented in detail.

Writing code that survives errors which may arise during run time is an art. There are multiple approaches to writing error-resistant code (we've already seen some examples of defensive code in previous chapters). The way programmers get good at creating error-free code is to learn by experience—no one is immune to syntax, logic, or run-time errors!

## Types of Errors

During the design and run time of nearly all applications, errors eventually occur. They fall into three categories:

- Syntax and compile-time errors. These arise due to typographical errors when you are entering code (typing Selct rather than Select), or forgetting to correctly structure logic blocks (for example an If block without a End If statement).

- Logic errors (Bugs!). This category can be the most frustrating to solve. Logic errors arise when your code fails to proceed according to your plans. For example, you may expect a variable to have some value in a particular portion of your code but have not considered situations where the variable may be empty when the code runs.

- Run-time errors. Those errors that arise due to a condition making your code invalid or incorrect. They appear only when the application is running. Your database may, as an example, expect a valid network connection while your code is running. A failure of the network falls into this category. Allowing a user to conduct a divide by zero operation is another example of a run-time error.

# Syntax Errors

Compile-time errors are due to incorrect syntax in your code. The VBA editor offers several facilities for preventing or correcting compile-time errors. Each of these facilities was introduced in Chapter 1.

- Automatic syntax checking. If you have automatic syntax checking turned on (and you should), Access will parse each sentence as you write. This eliminates the overall majority of compile-time errors before you run your code because Access flags most syntax errors immediately.

- Auto List Members. When this feature is turned on, Access will produce a list of all valid objects as you type and attempt to complete your entry. This feature eliminates misnaming objects and setting properties or methods that do not apply to that object.

- Auto Quick Info. This is a feature that will list the arguments for any valid sub or function available to you (including those you write and store in general modules). Like the Auto List Members feature, it prevents syntax errors and missing arguments when you refer to a procedure or function.

 To turn any of the above three features on, from within the VBA Editor, choose the **Tools** menu and then choose **Options**. Select the **Editor** tab and check the desired features.

# Compile-Time Errors

Some syntax checking cannot be done when you are writing code. Any program control structure such as **If Then Else** or **Select Case** that requires more than one line cannot be parsed by the VBA editor as you type. For these situations, use the **Compile** command. From the **Debug** menu, choose **Compile** *project name.* If you do not receive an error message the code in all open modules is free of syntax errors. The most common errors caught by this method include:

- Errors in the structure of logic blocks. For example a **Select Case** without an ending **End Select** statement.

- Undeclared variables when **Option Explicit** is enforced.

- References to unknown data types or unreferenced objects.

- Multiple declarations of a variable or object with the same name and within the same scope.

# Logic Errors

Logic errors arise due to mistakes in your logic about how the program should proceed. They can be difficult errors to troubleshoot as generally your code runs without triggering an error but you don't receive the expected result. The following code example illustrates a typical situation:

```
For I = 1 to 10
    if Me.Controls(1).Value = "Smith" Then
        MsgBox "Found the Target Value"
        Exit For
    End If
Next I
```

In the code example above, a **For Next** loop is used to step through the first ten controls on a form (here referred to using the **Me** keyword). If the value of one of the referenced controls is equal to the literal term *Smith*, a message box is displayed and program control exits the loop. The problem (which is part syntax error too) is that the *index* of the Me.Control object is *not* the incrementing variable, *I*, but the numeral *1*. Unless the first control contains the target value this code will not work as expected. Errors like this are surprisingly common. The human mind is very good at *not* seeing the 1 in the previous example and recognizing that an *I* is supposed to be there instead.

The next example illustrates another typical situation:

```
Private Sub cmdPrintReport_Click()
Select Case optReportType.Value
    Case 1
        strReportName = "rptEmployee"
    Case 2
        strReportName = "rptMailingLabels"
End Select
DoCmd.OpenReport strReportName
End Sub
```

In this code example we are assuming that the option group *optReportType* has a control that has been selected. It is possible to create an option group without a default choice and if the user opens such a form and selects the command button that fires this code an error will result. In this case, there is no report name and an error will occur when the DoCmd.OpenReport is called. The correct code in this example would include a **Case Else** block which would present a message box reminding the user to select a report first, then a command to **Exit Sub**. Alternatively, if a default value is hard-wired into the specification for the option group, a **Case Else** statement isn't required.

## Points on Troubleshooting Logic Errors

Troubleshooting code is as much art as it is technique. As you become more versed in writing code, you get better at anticipating errors that may arise, and you begin to write defensive code that anticipates errors. For beginners, however, there is the task of dealing with errors you have not seen before.

There are three major approaches to solving a logic error. You may need to use all three when troubleshooting your code:

- Test conditions fail because a variable is not the value you anticipated. This is a frequent situation because code typically has many places where test conditions are established (every **If Then**, **Select Case**, and **Do Loop** has test conditions). A useful troubleshooting technique is to place one or more breakpoints in your code then step through execution, reading the value of critical variables as you go along. Remember that any variable will display its value if the mouse pointer is positioned over it for more than a second. You can also move to the Immediate Window and issue the Print command, followed by the variable name, or open the **Locals Window** and/or the **Watches Window** and monitor variable values.

- Program flow is not what you expect. Situations that cause this type of error include premature exits, unexpected jumps to other procedures, or test conditions in control blocks yielding unanticipated results. Most developers use breakpoints and the various step commands to watch how program control moves through one or more procedures. If control jumps unexpectedly, you'll see it when stepping through the procedure. You can then investigate that portion of code to ensure that either test conditions or control statements are written correctly.

- Keywords or object attributes are not applied correctly. You may be using a keyword or an event, method, or property of an object inappropriately. As an example, you may have code in a form's *Activate* event to perform some startup task, but fail to understand that this event also fires every time focus leaves the form and returns to the form. The best tool for ensuring that you fully understand the keywords and objects you work with is on-line help. Developers spend a reasonable amount of time reading on-line help topics to fully understand the syntax and the usage of the significant components of their code. One common technique is to build test *scaffolding*—perhaps a couple of **MsgBox** objects in certain event handlers so you can understand when events fire. Once you've understood how program flow moves the **MsgBox** objects can be removed and replaced with the functional code.

## How to Work with Breakpoints

A breakpoint is a location within an executable portion of code that forces run time to halt and to enter *break mode*. Once stopped you can step one line through your code, read or change the value of variables, run to a specific location, step into or jump over sub or function procedures, or continue running the code. Breakpoints *may not* be established in a non-executing section of code. Thus blank lines, comments, and variable and object declarations may not be break points.

During break mode you can float the mouse over variable names and an **Auto Data Tip** will appear to indicate the current value of the variable. In many instances you can also edit sections of code, however, certain actions such as creating a new variable or resizing an array will cause the editor to cease execution and return to **Design Time**.

Step 1.    While in **Design Time**, position the insertion point on an executable line of code. Generally this should be before or at the beginning of a logic block or sub or function procedure you suspect is an issue.

Step 2.    Press *F9*, or click on the left margin of the code window, or on the **Debug** toolbar, then choose **Toggle Breakpoint**. A breakpoint in code will appear similar to the following:

```
Sub ListAllForms()

 Dim ctrl As Control
 Static bolToggle As Boolean

 For Each ctrl In Forms("frmStaffInfo").Controls
     If bolToggle = False Then
      ctrl.ForeColor = 4210752
     Else
      ctrl.ForeColor = 0
     End If
 Next

 bolToggle = Not bolToggle

 End Sub
```

Step 3.    Run your code (you may need to switch to Access and trigger your code using a form or report). When the target breakpoint is reached, code execution will break and the editor will appear as follows:

# Debug Menu Options

| Option | Description |
| --- | --- |
| Step Into  *F8* | Proceeds with code execution one line at a time. |
| Step Over  *Shift F8* | If on a line that calls a sub or function procedure, this command will run the sub or function procedure *without* entering that procedure in break mode. |
| Step Out  *Ctrl Shift F8* | If in a sub or function procedure, called from another section of code with a breakpoint, this command will complete the code within the current procedure without breaking and return to the original breakpoint in the calling procedure. |
| Run to Cursor  *Ctrl F8* | If the cursor has been placed elsewhere within the code during breakpoint, this command will execute the code between the current breakpoint and the cursor, then break at the cursor location. |
| Add Watch | Opens the **Add Watch** dialog. Watches were discussed on page 31. |
| Edit Watch | Opens the **Edit Watch** dialog. |
| Quick Watch  *Shift F9* | Presents information about the current variable or object. |
| Toggle Breakpoint  *F9* | Adds or removes a breakpoint at the current break or cursor location. |
| Clear All Breakpoints  *Ctrl Shift F9* | Clears all breakpoints from the project. |

Step 4.    Choose an option from the **Debug** menu (or use one of the shortcut keys) as discussed in the previous table.

Pressing *F5* while in break mode will return to run time. However if other breakpoints or untrapped errors are encountered, execution enters break mode again.

To change the value of a variable, position the cursor in the **Immediate window** and issue a reassignment command. Example: intCounter=45

VBA includes the **Stop** statement that will also cause code execution to enter break mode. Using **Stop** in code is considered poor form. Breakpoints don't survive closing a database file while **Stop** statements do. Unless you are careful to remove all **Stop** statements you can be in for a surprise once your code has entered production phase.

# Run Time Errors

Run time errors occur when your application is running. Some of these errors are in fact logic errors that arise as your code operates. Examples include:

- Operating system errors. A user fails to place a required CD or DVD in a disk drive when needed.

- Database errors. A user attempts to populate a field with the incorrect data type.

- Out of Range errors. A user enters two values that would permit your code to conduct a division by zero operation. This is not a permitted action in VBA.

This list goes on and on. Even seasoned programmers can be surprised by the things users attempt to do with their applications!

## Writing Defensive Code

There are two basic strategies for handing run time errors: defensive coding techniques and error handlers.

Defensive coding techniques anticipate places in your code where problems are likely to occur. You write code in these places to handle the problem automatically. In the function example below, the test of whether *HeadCount* is zero is a defensive technique. By setting *HeadCount* to a negative number, the result of the function is negative, flagging the developer to some problem with the variable values. If *HeadCount* entered the function as zero without this defense, a **Divide by zero** error would be raised, stopping program flow at the second to the last line of the function.

```
Function ProjectCostPerPerson (TotalProjectCost _
        As Currency, HeadCount As Integer) _
        As Currency

If HeadCount = 0 then HeadCount = -1
ProjectCostsPerPerson = TotalProjectCost / _
        HeadCount
End Function
```

## Points on Defensive Code

Knowing where you need to be particularly defensive helps in writing better code. Here are a few points to consider:

- Any place in your code where you prompt the user for input is a potential problem. Misspellings, incorrect keystrokes, and other issues cause developers to write defensive code to clean up such potentially dirty (or dangerous) data input.

- Arithmetic operations, especially division, can raise errors. As mentioned, divide by zero errors are common.

- Places where code interacts with the "real world" can generate errors. Prompting a user to save data to an external device when it isn't on or present, or sending a print job to a printer that is off line are both classic examples.

## Working with Error Handlers

Even the best defensive code sometimes misses an error and execution stops. Beyond writing good defensive code, the complementary approach is to include error handlers. An error handler is a special code structure you build at the procedure level to trap nearly any error condition that arises, including those error messages generated by Access. Error handlers use a series of VBA reserved keywords to work.

Developers use error handlers because:

- They give you control over all error messages. Thus you can "humanize" many of Access' more arcane messages.

- All trappable errors are caught. Thus you have the ability to keep your programming running even for unanticipated errors which might otherwise be fatal (e.g., shut your application down). Defensive code writing, although a useful technique, cannot trap most run-time errors.

# Error Handlers

An error handler is generally located within a procedure. There are three essential components of an error handler:

The first component is an initial line of code, which declares that an error handler is present and which either names the *line label* that identifies the beginning of the error handler,

```
On Error GoTo linelabel
```

Or instructs VBA to resume program flow on the next line following the one generating an error:

```
On Error Resume Next
```

The second component is a line of code *before* the error handler and *after* the procedure's general code, which permits program control to leave the procedure if no errors occurred.

```
Exit Sub|Function
```

If this component is omitted there isn't anything to stop program flow from entering the error handler!

Lastly, the line label, which indicates the starting point of the error handler. In VBA, line labels are any block of continuous text (no blank spaces) terminating in a colon. For example, a line named *PrintErrors* would appear as:

```
PrintErrors:
```

A sub or function procedure with an error handler would take a form similar to the following:

```
Sub PrintReport()
On Error GoTo PrintErrors

'normal procedure code would go here.

Exit Sub 'this is the exit point for "good" code

PrintErrors:
      'the error handler goes here

End Sub
```

When an error is trapped, program flow jumps to the error handler indicated by the line label mentioned in the **On Error** statement. Once program control is in an error handler you need to conduct two tasks:

- Determine the nature of the error. This is generally accomplished by probing properties of the **Err** object which stores information about the most recent VBA error in your project.

- React to the trapped error. Typical reactions may be to exit the procedure, attempt to fix the error and **Resume**, or issue a **Resume Next** command to start at a point immediately beyond the line which triggered the error.

# The Err Object

The Err object is a component of Visual Basic, although it interacts with Access whenever an error is raised and an error handler is present. The object has a few significant properties and methods which are outlined in the following table.

| Attribute | Description |
| --- | --- |
| Clear | This method clears all properties of the Err object. Generally this is not a required method as encountering any **Resume** statement also clears the Err object's properties. |
| Description | A text description of the error encountered. This is a property. |
| Number | A property that returns a number associated with any given error type. Generally, numbers below 255 are common errors of VBA and the operating system. Many specialized objects reserve numbers in the negative or high range (e.g.,-345534). |
| Source | A property that returns a string which returns the name of the application that generated the error. |
| Raise | A method used to emulate a particular error. The method takes a single argument, which is the error number. |

# The Resume Statement

Once an error has been raised and identified, you need to respond in some manner. There are several choices:

- Abandon the procedure altogether by exiting (**Exit Sub** or **Exit Function**).

- Stay in the procedure and fix the condition that raised the error and resume with the line that originally generated the error (**Resume**).

- Stay in the procedure and jump to the next line following the point where the error was generated (**Resume Next**).

- Jump to some named line in code. This point may or may not be in the same procedure (**Resume** *LineLabel*).

For all but the first option, you resume program execution by using the **Resume** keyword. There are several variations as outlined in the following table:

# Resume Statements

| Statement | Description |
| --- | --- |
| Resume | Continues program execution at the line that originally raised the error. You should include code to rectify the error condition first. |
| Resume Next | Program execution continues with the first line after the line that raised the error. |
| Resume *Linelabel* | Program execution is redirected to a line indicated by *Linelabel*. |

# Examples of Error Handlers

We will illustrate two general classes of errors: division by zero (or other errors that occur when an arithmetic operation is in progress) and interaction with the "real world"—in this case expecting a disk drive to exist and be ready.

## Divide by Zero—Inform and Quit

In the first case the example will assume that informing the user of a mistake fixes the issue. The code completes without failing and the user is returned to the starting point enabling one correct the data entry mistake and try again. The form, illustrated below, contains three two boxes (txtNumerator and txtDenominator) which receive input from the user, a label, lblAnswer (captioned as *Result*), that presents the result of the calculation, and a command button (captioned with the divisor symbol - / - and named cmdDivide).

The error handler responds to three common numeric errors: *Overflow* (the user enters a number beyond the range of the expected data type), *division by zero* (the main trappable error in this example), and *type mismatch* (occurs when data of the wrong data type is attempted to be loaded into a variable—for example entering a letter when a numeric value is expected). Because the real world can get interesting, the error handler includes a generic case that handles any unanticipated error. It formats a message that includes the error number, **Err.Number** and the description of the error, **Err.Description**. This is a useful technique as end users can inform the developer of the nature of the error. With this information the developer can include additional **Case** statements in future releases to more elegantly handle the currently unanticipated errors.

The code ends with a block that is identified by the line label *RecoverDivisionError* that presents an informative message to the user, clears the text boxes and results label, and then exits the routine.

The form appears as follows:

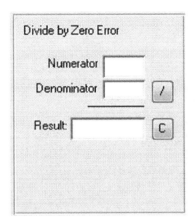

The code behind the form appears in the command button's Click event:

```vb
Private Sub cmdDivide_Click()

On Error GoTo RecoverDivisionError
    Dim Answer As Double
    Answer = txtNumerator / txtDenominator

    lblAnswer.Caption = Answer

    Exit Sub 'prevents code from entering the error handler
'begin error handler
DivisionErrorHandler:
    Dim strErrMsg As String

    Select Case Err.Number
        Case 6 'overflow
            strErrMsg = "An overflow error has occurred." & _
                " Either your numbers are too large or" & _
                " letters are being used."
            Resume RecoverDivisionError
```

```
      Case 11 'division by zero
        strErrMsg = "A division by zero error occurred." & _
           " Your denominator cannot be a zero!"
        Resume RecoverDivisionError
      Case 13 'type mismatch
        strErrMsg = "Either the numerator or denominator" & _
           " are not numbers or are out of range."
        Resume RecoverDivisionError
      Case Else 'all other errors
        strErrMsg = "An unknown or unanticipated error " & _
           " has occurred. Please contact the " & _
           " developer about this problem." & Err.Number & _
           " : " & Err.Description
        Resume RecoverDivisionError
    End Select
  Exit Sub 'End Error Handler

  'begin jump point from error handler for message/clean up
  RecoverDivisionError:
    'do some clean up to the display and leave the procedure
    MsgBox strErrMsg, vbOKOnly, "Error Handler Example"
    txtNumerator = ""
    txtDenominator = ""
    lblAnswer.Caption = " "
    Exit Sub

  End Sub
```

## Disk/Device Error—a Chance to Recover?

Dealing with the real world has its own issues. In this example the code counts the number of files (not folders) present in the root of a given file device. Errors that trigger as a result of a device not being present are handled conceptually like the division by zero error above. There isn't much you can do about them except inform the user of the problem and quit. When the device is present but the media isn't (diskette, CD/DVD, and other removal media drives) you can always offer to try again once the user has inserted the missing media. In this code example, we use the **Resume Next** statement in the error handler to process **Err.Number** 52 - Disk not Ready. The other known trappable error is **Err.Number** 5 which is triggered either when the device is not present (attempting to access Drive B: when one doesn't exist), or when the drive and media are present but no files exist. Lastly, the handler offers a generic case that, as in the previous example, presents a message and informs the user of the error number and description.

Notable in this example is the use of **Resume**. A message box appears that informs the user that the drive isn't ready. The **MsgBox** is formatted with a **Yes** or **No** button and a small decision structure processes the choices. If the user selects **No**, the code exits the procedure altogether. If **Yes** is selected, the **Resume** statement forces execution to rerun the line triggering the initial error.

A sample form appears below. Each of the command buttons calls a routine named **ReadDrive** and passes a drive letter as an expected argument. A label named *lblNumberofFiles* presents the result of the file count if no error occurs.

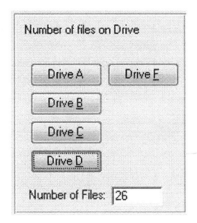

The code behind the *ReadDrive* procedure, called by each of the 5 command buttons, appears as:

```
Sub ReadDrive(DriveLetter As String)

On Error GoTo DriveReadError
Dim strErrMsg As String
Dim intCount As Integer
Dim intReply As Integer
Dim strDummyText As String
Me.lblNumberOfFiles.Caption = ""

'place a breakpoint on the next line to follow error
      processing.
strDummyText = Dir(DriveLetter, vbNormal)
intCount = intCount + 1
Do
  strDummyText = Dir
  intCount = intCount + 1
Loop While strDummyText <> ""

Me.lblNumberOfFiles.Caption = intCount

Exit Sub 'this prevents program execution from falling into
      the error handler

DriveReadError:
 Dim ErrorMessage As String
 Select Case Err.Number
  Case 5 'device unavailable or root directory empty
   strErrMsg = "The device is not available or there are no
      files in the root directory"
   MsgBox strErrMsg, vbOKCancel, "Error Handler Example"
   Exit Sub
  Case 52 'disk not ready
   strErrMsg = "There is no disk in the drive. Retry?"
   intReply = MsgBox(strErrMsg, vbYesNo, "Drive Error")
   If intReply = vbYes Then
     Resume
   Else 'response is vbNo
     Exit Sub
   End If
  Case Else 'all other errors
   strErrMsg = "Unknown or unanticipated error - " & _
      Err.Number & " : " & Err.Description
   MsgBox strErrMsg, vbOK, "Error Handler Example"
 End Select

End Sub
```

# Access Handles Errors Hierarchically

When Access encounters an error, it first looks for an error handler in the current procedure. If one is found the error is processed (according to your design of the handler). If no error handler is found, then Access moves up to the procedure that called the current procedure (if applicable) and checks for an error handler. Access will continue moving back through procedures in the *call stack* until it finds an error handler or it reaches the overlying form or report. At that point, an Access error is generated detailing the condition.

This behavior may cause problems because program control may end up in an error handler several procedures away from the actual point where the error occurred. Using breakpoints (see page 149) is a useful technique in this situation as you can follow the code and see the point where a jump to an error handler occurs.

 Many developers create highly compartmentalized code using numerous function and sub procedures, each assigned a specific task. *Unit Testing* is an approach where each of these procedures is systematically tested by feeding procedures bad or out-of-range data to ensure that the code was defensively written.

# Chapter 10 | The DAO and ADO Data Objects

## DAO and ADO

The object model first introduced on page 12 suggests that the tables and queries that make up an Access database are different from the other objects such as forms and reports. Access utilizes a special object, the ACE (Access Engine) to manage these structures and the data contained by tables. The ACE cannot be manipulated directly but it offers *interfaces* such as DAO and ADO which represent object-oriented approaches to programmatically controlling database data and database structure. DAO (Data Access Object) is the original technology and natively permits access to Microsoft Access databases via the ACE interface. ADO (ActiveX Data Object) is the newer technology and permits nearly universal access to ODBC (Open Database Connectivity) databases. You should consider what your programming needs are when working with these two technologies. Because DAO is native to Microsoft Access most programmers use it when needing to programmatically manipulate objects or data within Access databases. ADO is a broader technology that permits programmatic access to a wide variety of data sources, including server technology such as Microsoft SQL Server, Oracle, and MySQL. In this Chapter we will introduce both technologies. In Chapter 11 useful code examples will be provided.

### When to Use DAO

DAO (Data Access Objects) is the Microsoft technology that best maps the objects within the JET (Joint Engine Technology), which is the data engine for Microsoft Access. You would use DAO when:

- Your data access needs are exclusive to Microsoft Access databases. DAO interacts with an Access database natively and is therefore faster than using ADO connected to an Access database.

- You intend to create or modify tables or queries, or the relations that join such tables or queries.

- Your application needs to programmatically access the Microsoft Access Security model.

## When to Use ADO

ADO in its simplest form is purely involved in data access. You can, by including an additional library, add the ability to create and modify tables and queries in Microsoft Access databases. You would use ADO when:

- Your application requires connection to data not stored in an Access database.

- The target database may be migrated to a different platform. As long as data remain in one of the supported databases, your code will require only minor modification to continue running.

- Your application requires a smaller footprint in memory. The ADO library is much smaller than the DAO library.

# Library References

You may need to establish a library reference before working with either DAO or ADO. You can check to ensure that the DAO library has been automatically referenced by entering a line of code somewhere in your project such as:

```
Dim db As DAO.Database
```

If **Auto List Members** lists the **DAO** object and then lists its members, the library is already referenced. If not, you need to add a reference to the DAO library.

To check whether the ADO library is already referenced in your project, you can conduct a similar test by entering a line of code such as:

```
Dim cnn As ADODB.Connection
```

Again, if the ADO library has been attached **Auto List Members** will correctly show all members of the **ADODB** object. If **Auto List Members** fails to list these members you'll need to add a reference to the ADO library.

## Managing Library References

There are several libraries for both DAO and ADO objects. To add or remove a library reference you must be in the VBA code editor.

Step 1.    From the **Tools** menu, choose **References**. The **References** dialog box will appear similar to the following:

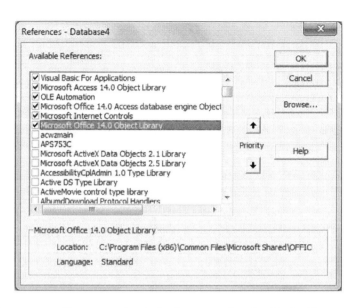

Step 2.     To remove a library, uncheck the box associated with the library name. Note that any objects in your code that use this library must be removed or compile-time errors will occur.

Step 3.     To add a library, first locate the desired file and then add a check next to the library name. You may add multiple libraries (including both DAO and ADO libraries if you wish to use both technologies concurrently). Use the following table as a guide:

| Library | Description |
| --- | --- |
| **Microsoft Office XX Access Database Engine Object Library** | A version of the DAO object library available to all members of the Office Suite. |
| **Microsoft DAO X.X Object Library** | The core DAO object library. If the library above is referenced, you do not need to include this reference. |
| **Microsoft ADO Ext. X for DDL and Security** | Provides references to the tables, users and groups in an Access database, thus adding similar functionality as found in the DAO object library. |
| **Microsoft ActiveX Data Objects X.X Library** | The core ADO object library. |
| **Microsoft ActiveX Data Objects (Multidimensional) XX** | An add on that permits programmatic access to data cubes via ADO. |

Step 4.     Choose **OK** when done.

In the previous table, XX and X.X refer to version numbers. In general you should work with the most recent (e.g. highest) version number available.

# The DAO Object Model

You can learn much about the functionality of any object hierarchy by studying its object model. The following illustration shows the model for the DAO. Collections are indicated by shading and plural names. Objects are not shaded in this diagram.

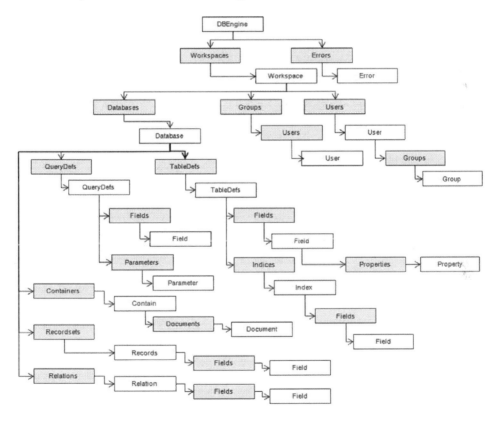

A brief look at this figure is an exploration of the data side of a Microsoft Access database. The essential path follows these objects: **DBEngine - Workspaces - Workspace - Databases - Database**. The last object is also accessed in VBA using the **CurrentDB** method. The **Database** object houses information about the structure and data in an Access database as outlined in the following table.

# Database Object Members

| Object | Description |
|---|---|
| TableDefs | A collection of **TableDef** objects, which store information about the structure of each table. When you work in **Table Design View** you are essentially manipulating a **TableDef** object. |
| QueryDefs | Like the **TableDefs** collection but for queries. Creating or modifying a query in **Query Design View** is essentially working with a **QueryDef** object. |
| Relations | A collection that stores information about the individual **Relations** in the database. The **Relationship Window** is the utility that manipulates **Relation** objects. |
| Recordsets | Manages the **Recordset** objects, which provide direct access to the data stored in the tables in the database. A **TableDef** houses information about the *structure* of a table while a **Recordset** provides access to the data contained by a table. |
| Containers | This collection houses information about the ownership and permissions for objects within the database. |

# Features of Data Access Using DAO

Of the two data access technologies being discussed, DAO permits direct access to the Microsoft Access Engine (or ACE). This engine manages the tables, queries, indices, and relations that make up an Access database. Thus, DAO is a good technology if you need to access or modify the structure of a table, query, index or relation within Access. It is also a good model if you need to programmatically manipulate data that is native to Microsoft Access.

## Using DAO to Access Table Structure

Knowing something about Access and this object model should enable you to predict certain facts. For example, the **Field** object of the **Fields** collection for a **TableDef** probably contains properties that house all the information accessible for the field while in **Table Design View**. As proof of concept, consider the following image of the **Table Design Editor** for a table named *tblStaffInfo* and focused on the attributes of a field named *StartDate*:

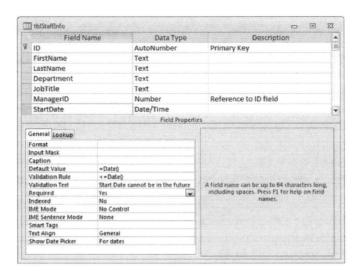

Now consider the following VBA code which enumerates through the **Properties** collection of the **Field Object** for the *StartDate* field contained within the *tblStaffInfo* **TableDef** object:

```
Sub DAO_Example()
On Error Resume Next

Dim tbl As DAO.TableDef
Dim prp As Property
Dim db  As DAO.Database

Set db = CurrentDb

Set tbl = db.TableDefs("tblStaffInfo")
  For Each prp In tbl.Fields("StartDate").Properties
    Debug.Print prp.Name, prp.Value
  Next

End Sub
```

Compare some of the field attributes illustrated in the previous graphic with a screen shot of part of the output in the **Immediate** window following code execution:

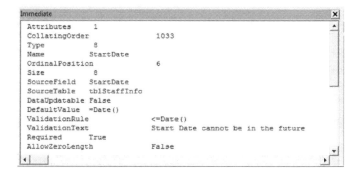

```
Immediate                                                              ×
  Attributes      1
  CollatingOrder                      1033
  Type            8
  Name            StartDate
  OrdinalPosition                     6
  Size            8
  SourceField     StartDate
  SourceTable     tblStaffInfo
  DataUpdatable   False
  DefaultValue    =Date()
  ValidationRule                      <=Date()
  ValidationText                      Start Date cannot be in the future
  Required        True
  AllowZeroLength                     False
```

We will explore the power of the DAO object, especially as it relates to working with **TableDef** and **Recordset** objects in the next chapter.

## Using DAO to Access Table Data

DAO is the preferred technology if you need to work with table data stored either in the current database or in another Microsoft Access database. You only need to instantiate two objects, one representing a copy of the current database and another to work with the table data. In the following brief code fragment the values from two fields, *FirstName* and *LastName*, contained in a table named *tblStaffInfo* in the current database are dumped to the **Immediate Window**. Line numbers have been added for discussion following the example.

```
     Sub DAO_Example()
1.   Dim db As Database
2.   Dim rec As Recordset

3.   Set db = Application.CurrentDb

4.   Set rec = db.OpenRecordset("tblStaffInfo")
5.   rec.MoveFirst
6.   Do
7.       Debug.Print rec![LastName]
8.       rec.MoveNext
9.   Loop Until rec.EOF

10.  rec.Close
11.  Set rec = Nothing
12.  Set db = Nothing
     End Sub
```

| Line | Description |
|---|---|
| 1,2 | Establishes references to two object variables of the DAO **Database** and **Recordset** objects. |
| 3,4 | Instantiates the two objects (In lines 1 and 2 they were only defined). Line 4 not only sets a reference to a **Recordset** object, but specifically to the table *tblStaffInfo* using the **OpenRecordset** method of the **Database** object. |
| 5 | Forces the *cursor* to move to the first record in the recordset. |
| 6, 9 | We enter a standard **Do..Loop** with the exit condition at the bottom of the loop. When the cursor moves beyond the last record in the table, the **EOF** (end of file) property of the **Recordset** object is set to *True*. |
| 7 | The code prints the values of two fields in the **Immediate Window**. As the loop proceeds, the cursor is moved to the next record in the table as a result of the next line. |
| 8 | The **MoveNext** method of the **Recordset** object tells the database server to position the cursor to the next record. If you omit this line the code will enter an infinite loop as the **EOF** property of the **Recordset** will never become *True*! |
| 10 | Closes the recordset object. |
| 11, 12 | De-instantiates both DAO objects. This task is good programming practice as it fully releases all resources associated with these objects. Note that once **End Sub** is reached, VBA *should* de-instantiate all objects and variables. That said, formally issuing this command ensures that memory resources are released. |

# The ADO Object Model

Whereas the DAO gives you direct access to the data side of an Access database, the ActiveX Data Object (ADO) has a different purpose. It was designed to provide developers with near universal ability to connect to other data sources. Any database which complies with the Open Database Connectivity (ODBC) standard may be accessed using ADO. In many cases, just changing the value of the **Connection** object will permit you to switch between database providers. For example if your data migrates from a Microsoft SQL Server database to a MySQL database, you would change the **ConnectionString** property of the **Connection** object. If your SQL statements are understood by both servers the migration only requires that a single property change.

The simplicity of the ADO object can be seen in its object model as illustrated below:

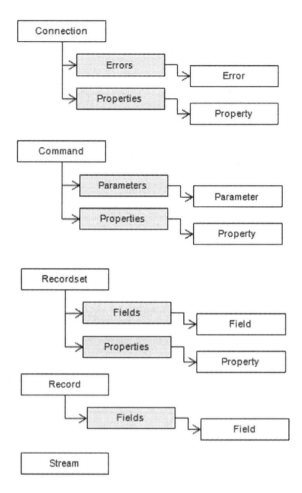

The most obvious feature of the ADO object model is how non-hierarchical it is. There are 5 top-level objects that are not members of a higher level object. This is in stark contrast to the DAO model. The ADO top-level objects are outlined in the following table:

# ADO Object Members

| Object | Description |
|---|---|
| Connection | Mediates a connection with a data provider. In a client-server environment this object represents an actual network connection to the server. |
| Command | This object allows you to issue SQL commands via the **Connection** object to manipulate the structure of the database, conduct bulk operations, or return records into a **Recordset** object. |
| Recordset | Represents an entire table or the results of a query as mediated through the **Command** object. A **Recordset** only references a single row at a time, although you use specific methods of the object to move between records. |
| Record | Represents a single record within a **Recordset**. If the data provider only returns a single record it may be returned as a **Record** object rather than as a **Recordset**. |
| Stream | This object manages a stream of binary data, either from a document or folder within a file system, or from a **Record** object. |

# Features of Data Access Using ADO

ADO is a lightweight technology that permits developers working in a variety of Microsoft languages (Visual Basic, VBA, C++, etc.) to connect programmatically to several different data sources, including Access (via the JET engine), Microsoft SQL Server, Microsoft Active Directory Service, Oracle databases, MySQL, IBM DB2, and other ODBC-compliant databases.

The ADO object model is relatively simple.

- You utilize a **Connection** object to open and manage communication between your application and the remote data source. **Connection** objects are mandatory in ADO. You cannot reference a **Command**, **Recordset**, **Record**, **Error**, or **Stream** object without a valid **Connection** object already established.

- A Command object delivers SQL commands from your application to the remote database. Its use is not required if you intend to manipulate or view returned records using a **Recordset** object. However, using the **Command** object makes sense if you intend to issue action query commands such as DELETE or UPDATE, or Data Definition Language commands such as CREATE TABLE.

- If a result of the **Command** object returns results, you will need to use a **Recordset** object to manipulate the returned results.

- Any errors raised by the remote database during execution of your **Command** objects are stored in a collection of **Error** objects.

- The **Recordset** object can connect to an entire table, or use can use SQL statements to filter the returned results.

## Using ADO to Connect to a Data Source

ADO requires a **Connection** object at a minimum. Once a connection has been established, you can manipulate **Command**, **Recordset**, **Record**, and **Stream** objects. When you connect to a data source (including Microsoft Access) you must reference a driver, which is a file normally installed on your computer that mediates the connection between your code and the target database. Drivers are usually provided by the database vendor and are operating system specific. For example, if you are running a Microsoft Windows operating system and wish to connect to a MySQL database (the operating system that the MySQL server is running on is immaterial), you would first visit the MySQL website and download a driver specific for Windows that uses ODBC. The latter point is important as many vendors offer several driver options. For MySQL, these include .NET, Java, Python, and C++ drivers. You install a driver in the same way you would install an executable program. Drivers are managed using the ODBC Database Administrator application (accessed in Windows through the Control Panel).

Once the appropriate driver has been installed, you connect to the target database in one of two basic ways. The most straightforward is to include reference to the driver, server, database, user and password within a **ConnectionString** property. This approach is completely mediated within your code, although the downside is that sensitive information such as username and password are potentially exposed to non-privileged users. An example of such a connection string is presented below:

```
Dim cnn As ADODB.Connection
Set cnn = New ADODB.Connection
cnn.ConnectionString = cnn.ConnectionString = "Driver=MySQL
      ODBC 5.1 Driver; Server=93.184.216.119;
      Database=codelibrary; Uid=user; Pwd=P@$$w0rd;"
cnn.Open
```

The arguments required vary by database provider but at a minimum you must reference a driver and reference the database server, either by name or location (which can be on a local network or via the Internet). Most database servers will require additional information such as the database you wish to connect to and username and password credentials.

The second approach involves establishing a *Data Source Name* using the Windows ODBC Database Administrator (this process is discussed in Appendix B). The usefulness of this second approach is that the connection can be tested to ensure that all components work correctly and the user name and password required to connect to the database is hidden from view.

In the following code example, a DSN has been established and tested and given the name *MySQL_Ubuntu*. The connection string using this approach would appear as:

```
Dim cnn As ADODB.Connection
Set cnn = New ADODB.Connection
cnn.ConnectionString = "DSN=MySQL_Ubuntu"
cnn.Open
```

## Using ADO to Access Records

This is the most common use of ADO—to read data from another database (we will discuss issuing SQL commands and writing data in Chapter 11). There are a couple of approaches you can use. In the most streamlined form you establish a **Connection** object, then call the **Open** method of a **Recordset** object. In the examples that follow, we'll assume that a table exists on another database server named *tblStateCodes*. This table contains two text fields, *StateName* and *StateCode* and in these examples is populated with the US state names and US postal codes for states generally considered to be in the mid-Atlantic portion of the East Coast.

An approach using only a **Connection** and **Recordset** object would appear similar to the following (line numbers have been added for the following discussion):

```
    Sub ADO_Example()
1.  Dim cnn As ADODB.Connection
2.  Dim rec As ADODB.Recordset

3.  Set cnn = New ADODB.Connection
4.  Set rec = New ADODB.Recordset

5.  cnn.Open "DSN=MySQL_Ubuntu"
6.  rec.Open "tblStateCodes", cnn, adOpenForwardOnly
7.      With rec
8.          .MoveFirst
9.          Do
10.             Debug.Print ![StateName], ![StateCode]
11.            .MoveNext
12.         Loop Until rec.EOF
13.     End With
14. rec.Close
15. cnn.Close
16. Set rec = Nothing
17. Set cnn = Nothing
    End Sub
```

The output in the **Immediate Window** once this code is run would appear as:

The following table explains the code line by line.

| Line | Description |
|---|---|
| 1,2 | Establishes references to two object variables of the ADODB **Connection** and **Recordset** objects. |
| 3,4 | Instantiates the two objects. In lines 1 and 2 they were only defined. |
| 5 | A call to the **Open** method of the **Connection** object establishes a valid connection. Here the connection references an existing DSN rather than working with the **ConnectionString** property. |
| 6 | A **Recordset** object is populated with data. The **Open** method here takes three arguments: the name of the table to open (this could also have been a SQL SELECT statement with a WHERE clause, if desired). The second argument references the current **Connection** object. The last argument tells the distant database server how the *cursor* should behave. In this case the intrinsic constant *adOpenForwardOnly* tells the server that we intend to only access records moving from first to last. Another common cursor value is *adOpenDynamic* which permits cursor movement back and forth within the table. |
| 7,13 | The **With..End With** reserved word pair just establishes a reference to the *rec* object. Between these two lines the code references *rec* without actually naming it. |
| 8 | The **MoveFirst** method of the **Recordset** object moves the cursor on the distant database server to the beginning of the table. |
| 9,12 | We enter a standard **Do..Loop** with the exit condition at the bottom of the loop. When the cursor moves beyond the last record in the table, the **EOF** (end of file) property of the **Recordset** object is set to *True*. |
| 10 | The code prints the values of two fields in the **Immediate Window**. As the loop proceeds, the cursor is moved to the next record in the table as a result of the next line. |
| 11 | The **MoveNext** method of the **Recordset** object tells the distant database server to position the cursor to the next record. If you omit this line the code will enter an infinite loop as the **EOF** property of the **Recordset** will never become *True*! |
| 14,15 | Closes the **Recordset** and **Connection** objects. |
| 16,17 | De-instantiates both ADO objects. This task is good programming practice as it fully releases all resources associated with these objects. Note that once **End Sub** is reached, VBA *should* de-instantiate all objects and variables. That said, formally issuing this command ensures that memory resources are released. |

Another approach initializes a **Command** object, then establishes the **ActiveConnection** and **CommandText** properties before calling the **Execute** method. This method is used to essentially populate the **Recordset** object with the results of the **CommandText** property. After this point the code behaves identically to the previous example in terms of cycling through the returned results.

```
Dim cnn As ADODB.Connection
Dim cmd As ADODB.Command
Dim rec As ADODB.Recordset

Set cnn = New ADODB.Connection
Set cmd = New ADODB.Command
Set rec = New ADODB.Recordset

cnn.Open "DSN=MySQL_Ubuntu"

cmd.CommandText = "SELECT StateName, StateCode FROM
    tblStateCodes;"
cmd.ActiveConnection = cnn
Set rec = cmd.Execute

With rec
    .MoveFirst
    Do
        Debug.Print ![StateName], ![StateCode]
        .MoveNext
    Loop Until rec.EOF
    rec.Close
End With
```

The **Close** and **Set Nothing** statements would be the same as in the previous code example.

# Cursors and Recordsets

A cursor is essentially an entity that points to the current record when working with a recordset. Cursors are not encountered when you work with the Access user interface (except it may be useful to think of the current record indicator in table or query datasheet view as a cursor), but they are essential when using a data access technology such as DAO or ADO to view or manipulate recordsets. There are 4 cursor types that specify how you can view or manipulate data, as outlined in the following two tables:

# DAO Cursor Types

| Constant | Description |
| --- | --- |
| dbOpenDynamic | This is analogous to opening a *Dynamic* cursor in ADO. |
| dbOpenDynaset | The *Keyset* cursor in ADO. If you are connecting to any other data source except Access (i.e. you are using ODBC), this is the default cursor type. |
| dbOpenForwardOnly | The *Forward Only* cursor in ADO. |
| dbOpenSnapshot | Analogous to the *Static* ADO cursor. |
| dbOpenTable | Unique to DAO when working with an Access table. This cursor type is based directly on a table rather than the other cursor types, which are based on a query (even if you specify the table by name without using SQL). This is the default cursor type when you use DAO to connect to an Access database. |

# ADO Cursor Types

| Cursor | Description |
| --- | --- |
| Forward Only | You may only move forward in the recordset, from first to last record. The recordset does not synchronize with changes other users may make to the underlying data. This cursor type is memory efficient and record access is quick. |
| Static | Provides a static image of the underlying data. You can move in either direction through the recordset. Changes others may make to the data are not seen in this static view. In ADO, a static cursor may only reside on the client, not on the server. |
| Keyset | Permits movement in either direction through a recordset and also shows updates to data others may have changed. Records added by other users are not available. |
| Dynamic | This option supports both full motion through the recordset and updates that other users may make to the underlying data, *including* the addition of new records. This option consumes the greatest memory resources of any of the cursor types. |

When working with ADO, the cursor type is specified as an argument in the **Open** method. DAO doesn't specifically recognize enumerated cursor types, rather, by specifying a *Recordset Type* as the second argument when you call the **OpenRecordset** method of the **Database** object, you set the cursor.

## Locating the Cursor

Choosing a specific cursor type is one way to optimize performance when working with distant servers or very large datasets. In addition to the cursor type, both DAO and ADO permit you to specify *where* the cursor is located. In both technologies the default location is on the distant database server. In some cases, especially when working over a heavily loaded network or when working with a busy server and a relatively small data set, specifying that the cursor be local can result in performance improvements, although generally you can only work with static records.

ADO uses a simple and straightforward scheme for cursor location. The property, **CursorLocation** is a member of either the **Connection** or the **Recordset** object. In DAO, cursor location is specified as the **DefaultCursorDriver** property of the **Workspace** object. The choices are outlined below:

# DAO Cursor Location

| Constant | Description |
| --- | --- |
| **dbUseClientBatchCursor** | Required for any batch update operations. The cursor is managed on the client computer. |
| **dbUseDefaultCursor** | Defaults to using a server-side cursor. |
| **dbUseNoCursor** | No cursor is created. This results in a recordset of forward only, read only attributes. For small datasets this optimizes local performance. |
| **dbUseODBCCursor** | Creates a server-side cursor that is optimized for SQL statements that contain nested SELECT statements. In fact, this type of query must use this cursor type. |
| **dbUseServerCursor** | Forces the cursor to be located on the server. |

# ADO Cursor Location

| Constant | Description |
| --- | --- |
| **adUseServer** | The default cursor location is on the server side. |
| **adUseClient** | This value forces the cursor to be managed on the client side. |

In both technologies, if you intend on defining the cursor location this *must* occur prior to opening a **Recordset** (in ADO) or establishing a **connection** (in DAO). Once a connection or recordset has been established, enforcing a different cursor type or location has no effect.

### Troubleshooting Cursors

Using the incorrect cursor type can cause errors to arise under certain conditions. The most common being an attempt to move back through a recordset when the cursor is forward only, or attempting to update or add records when the cursor specifies a snapshot or static recordset.

If errors arise when you attempt to move back through a recordset, update an existing record, or add an additional record, ensure that you aren't using a restrictive cursor type. Remember than in DAO the cursor type is specified as the type of recordset you open. In either technology, you can try working with the least restrictive (but most resource-consuming) cursor type to see if the error condition clears. In ADO use the *Dynamic* cursor while in DAO open the recordset as *dbOpenDynamic*.

If performance issues arise it is generally because you are requesting a large recordset from a busy server or across an overloaded network. You can try forcing the cursor on the server side since working with a client side cursor forces the entire result set to be downloaded to the client computer and that can affect performance. The alternative approach is to reconsider your strategy and issue SQL statements that filter the recordset down to more manageable chunks of data. Nearly every flavor of SQL contains some syntax such as **LIMIT** and **OFFSET** that permits you to request "pages" of data.

# The ADOX Object Model

Unlike the DAO object model, the ADO model previously introduced only manages data containing objects such as tables and queries. If you need to manipulate the structure of a database (creating a new table for example) you use the ADOX object library. We will illustrate the object model here and introduce how to use these objects to create a new table and a new database in the next chapter.

The ADOX object model is used to create databases, tables, and to manage users, groups, stored procedures and views.

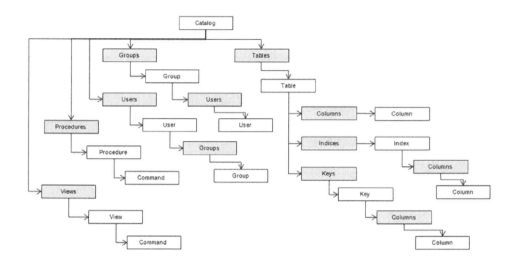

# Chapter 11 | Common Tasks Using Data Access

The previous Chapter focused on the object model for both DAO and ADO and outlined when each technology is best applied. Here, we will review some basics such as establishing connections and cycling through records and then move on to more advanced topics such as migrating data and creating tables and databases programmatically.

## DAO and ADO Basics

Both technologies require that you establish a connection, either to the current database or to a remote database. In the latter case, the remote database may be another Microsoft Access database, or it may be an ODBC-compliant database server. We will review all three scenarios for both technologies.

### Establishing a Connection to the Current Database

If your code is running in an Access database, establishing a **Connection** object is easy:

**Using DAO**

```
Dim db    As DAO.Database
Set db = CurrentDb
```

**Using ADO**

```
Dim cnnDb  As ADODB.Connection
Set cnnDb = CurrentProject.Connection
```

### Establishing a Connection to a Remote Access Database

When making a remote database connection, you must provide a value to the connection object's Provider property and then call the connection's Open method. The Open method requires the specifications to locate the database file.

**Using DAO**

```
Dim db     As DAO.Database
Set db = OpenDatabase("C:\Temp\MyData.accdb")
```

### Using ADO to Connect to an Access Database Prior to Access 2010

```
Dim cnnDb  As ADODB.Connection
Set cnnDb = New ADODB.Connection
cnnDb.Provider = "Microsoft.Jet.OLEDB.4.0"
cnnDb.Open "C:\My Documents\Remote Access Data.mdb"
```

### Using ADO to Connect to an Access Database Version 2010 or Later

```
Dim cnnDb  As ADODB.Connection
Set cnnDb = New ADODB.Connection
cnnDb.Provider = "Microsoft.ACE.OLEDB.12.0"
cnnDb.Open "C:\My Documents\Remote Access Data.accdb"
```

## Establishing a Connection to a Remote ODBC Data Source

Chapter 10 provides an example of using the **ConnectionString** property in ADO. Using a data source name (DSN) is the preferred method as connection passwords are hidden and you can test the connection when you create the DSN. Creating a DSN is covered in Appendix B.

### Using DAO to Connect to an ODBC Data Source

In this example, a DSN named *MySQL_Ubuntu* is assumed to exist on the local computer:

```
Dim db As DAO.Database
Set db = OpenDatabase("", dbDriverNoPrompt, False,
     "ODBC;DSN=MySQL_Ubuntu")
```

 On-line help for the **OpenDatabase** method suggests that the second and third argument are optional when establishing a DSN-based connection. They are not and in fact unless the second argument is the intrinsic constant *adDriverNoPrompt* a **Select Datasource** dialog box will appear. Note that although the first argument is required, passing an empty string is acceptable as long as the fourth argument contains the name of a valid DSN.

# Reading Table Data

Once you have established a connection to a recordset, both DAO and ADO require that you issue the **MoveNext** method to actually step through records. Both technologies also provide the **EOF** (end of file) property to signal when the last record is reached. Recordsets also recognize the **MovePrevious**, **MoveFirst**, and **MoveLast** methods, although the first two may generate errors if you are not using the appropriate cursor type with the current recordset.

## Opening a Recordset and Cycling Through all Records

In both code examples, it is assumed that the code is referring to a table in the current database.

### Using DAO

```
Dim db As Database
Dim rec As RecordSet
Set db = CurrentDB
Set rec = db.OpenRecordSet("Table name"),,,,

rec.MoveFirst
do
    Debug.Print rec![Field name]
    rec.MoveNext
Loop Until rec.EOF

Set rec = Nothing
Set db = Nothing
```

### Using ADO

```
Sub ADOReadLocalTable()
Dim cnnDb  As ADODB.Connection
Dim rec    As ADODB.Recordset

Set cnnDb = CurrentProject.Connection
Set rec = New ADODB.Recordset
rec.Open "[Employees]", cnnDb, adOpenKeyset, adLockOptimistic

rec.MoveFirst
Do
  Debug.Print rec![EmployeeID], _
        rec![LastName]
  rec.MoveNext
Loop Until rec.EOF

Set rec = Nothing
Set cnnDb = Nothing

End Sub
```

## Opening a Remote Access Database

Because DAO can access Microsoft JET-based databases natively, opening a remote Access database is somewhat simpler in DAO.

### Using DAO

```
Dim db As DAO.Database

Set db = OpenDatabase("C:\My Documents\Remote Access
    Data.accdb")
```

### Using ADO

```
Dim cnnDb As ADODB.Connection
Dim rec  As ADODB.Recordset
Set cnnDb = New ADODB.Connection
cnnDb.Provider = "Microsoft.ACE.OLEDB.12.0"
cnnDb.Open "C:\My Documents\Remote Access Data.mdb"
```

## Applying a Sort Order to the Recordset

To apply a sort order, you *must* specify that you wish to use the client cursor engine rather than the default local cursor engine. The client (provider) will return the sorted records into the local record set. In this example (similar to the preceding code) the records are sorted by [InvoiceDate].

```
Sub ADOSortRemoteRecords()
Dim cnnDb  As ADODB.Connection
Dim rec    As ADODB.Recordset

' Use connection to a remote Access database
Set cnnDb = New ADODB.Connection
cnnDb.Provider = "Microsoft.Jet.OLEDB.4.0"
cnnDb.Open "C:\My Documents\Remote Access Data.mdb"

Set rec = New ADODB.Recordset
'MUST USE THIS LINE TO RUN THE SORT PROPERTY!!!
rec.CursorLocation = adUseClient
rec.Open "[Invoices]", cnnDb, adOpenKeyset, adLockOptimistic
rec.Sort = "[InvoiceDate]"

rec.MoveFirst
Do
  Debug.Print rec![InvNbr], rec![Company], rec![InvoiceDate]
  rec.MoveNext
Loop While Not rec.EOF

Set rec = Nothing
Set cnnDb = Nothing

End Sub
```

Relying on the **Sort** property in either ADO or DAO can cause problems as the cursor type and location both play into whether a recordset can be sorted. It is far preferable to sort based on the SQL **ORDER BY** clause. There are two strong arguments for using this approach. First, the recordset is sorted while being created, not afterward. Second, ORDER BY is enforced by the distant database server and in the case of production servers such as Microsoft SQL Server, Oracle, or MySQL, these servers are optimized to perform sorting operations. The previous highlighted code would be rewritten as:

```
Rec.Open "SELECT * FROM [Invoices] ORDER BY [InvoiceDate]",
     cnnDB, adOpenKeyset
```

## Limiting the Results in a Recordset

You can pass SQL statements to the provider, which serve to return only a subset of the data. In either technology this can be accomplished by issuing a valid SQL statement with an appropriate WHERE clause when you open the **Recordset**. Additionally, in ADO you can also issue a SELECT statement using the **CommandText** property of the **Command** object.

As in the previous discussion, such a SELECT statement is issued in lieu of simply naming the table to open. The strong argument for this approach, rather than pulling all table data into the client and filtering locally is parallel to the argument for sorting. Production database servers are optimized to filter data using SQL statements, thus it makes sense to filter on the server and not at the client. The other obvious benefit is not having to move larger than required record sets across the network.

## Editing Table Data

Making changes to existing data or adding new records to a table constitute an edit operation. Both technologies require that you use an editable recordset and that you define how records are to be locked. Locking is used in multi-user environments to control how a single record is treated if two or more users attempt simultaneous edits. Locks usually are not an issue in Access but certainly are important when you use DAO or ADO to access records on a production database server.

In both technologies, locks are applied when you open a **Recordset**. The intrinsic constants and their meaning are described below:

## Recordset Lock Options

| Lock | Description |
| --- | --- |
| **dbOptimistic (DAO)** <br> **adLockOptimistic (ADO)** | Used when you expect the probability of concurrent edits is low. Locks only occur when the **Update** method of the recordset is called. |
| **dbOptimisticBatch (DAO)** <br> **adLockBatchOptimistic (ADO)** | For ODBC connections only and used when processing edits in batch mode. When editing large numbers of records this is an efficient lock mode. |
| **dbOptimisticValue (DAO)** | Locks only the record being edited, otherwise similar to Optimistic locking. Only available in DAO. |
| **dbPessimistic (DAO)** <br> **adLockPessimistic (ADO)** | Locks all records associated with the current recordset. For large tables in heavily used environments this type of lock can prevent many other users from working with the data until your code completes. |
| **adLockReadOnly (ADO)** | Indicates that the recordset may be not edited. |

When the lock type for a given recordset is not appropriate for an edit operation the ensuing error message will generally indicate that the operation isn't supported. This should serve as a clue that you need to reconsider what lock type is being applied.

## Adding a New Record

Adding a record is identical using either DAO or ADO. You begin the operation by calling the **AddNew** method of the recordset, then you populate fields. Once ready, you call the **Update** method to complete the operation.

**Adding a New Record Using DAO:**

```
Dim db As DAO.Database
Dim rec As DAO.Recordset

Set db = CurrentDb
Set rec = db.OpenRecordset("tblHRData", dbOpenTable,
    dbAppendOnly, dbOptimistic)
With rec
    .AddNew
    ![FirstName] = "Mary"
    ![LastName] = "Delacroix"
    ![Department] = "Management"
    ![JobTitle] = "Assistant"
    ![StartDate] = "03 September 2014"
    .Update
End With

rec.Close
Set rec = Nothing
Set db = Nothing
```

**Adding a New Record Using ADO:**

```
Dim cnn As ADODB.Connection
Dim rec As ADODB.Recordset

Set cnn = CurrentProject.Connection
Set rec = New ADODB.Recordset

rec.Open "tblHRData", cnn, adOpenDynamic, adLockOptimistic

With rec
    .AddNew
    ![FirstName] = "Joseph"
    ![LastName] = "d'Assandro"
    ![Department] = "IT"
    ![JobTitle] = "Programmer"
    ![StartDate] = "10/15/2013"
    .Update
End With

rec.Close
Set rec = Nothing
Set db = Nothing
```

 If the table contains an autonumber or auto increment field (as a primary key, for example) you should not attempt to enforce a value into that field. The database (including Access) will automatically assign a value once the **Update** method is called.

## Editing an Existing Record

The following code fragment illustrates how to change a field value in an open record set. The approach differs slightly between DAO and ADO in that DAO requires that you begin the edit by calling the **Edit** method of the **Recordset**. In both technologies, when you are ready to commit the edit you call the **Update** method for the **Recordset**.

**In DAO:**

```
rec.MoveFirst
Do

   If rec![CurrencyName] = "Franc" Then
      rec.Edit
      rec![CurrencyName] = "Euro"
      rec.Update
   End If
   rec.MoveNext
Loop While Not rec.EOF
```

**In ADO:**

```
rec.MoveFirst
Do

   If rec![CurrencyName] = "Franc" Then
      rec![CurrencyName] = "Euro"
      rec.Update
   End If
   rec.MoveNext
Loop While Not rec.EOF
```

## Committing an Edit

If you conduct an edit such as in the example above and you either:

- Move entirely through the recordset to its end, or

- Close the recordset, or

- Call the **Update** method.

The changes are committed to the underlying table.

There are two strategies for rolling back an edit. For an edit to a single record use the **CancelUpdate** method of the **Recordset** object. In both technologies this *must* occur before the **Update** method is called, so **CancelUpdate** is generally used in the context of an error handler.

The other approach is to wrap a series of edits (or additions as this approach applies to both actions) within a *transaction*.

## Working with Transactions

A transaction is an all-or-none method of editing table data where the individual edits or record additions are wrapped within a **BeginTrans..CommitTrans** block. To cancel a transaction you call the **Rollback** (DAO) or the **RollbackTrans** (ADO) method. A major difference between the two data access technologies is which object manages transactions. In DAO a transaction is a method of the **Workspace** object and thus you must formally instantiate a **Workspace**. In ADO, transactions are managed by the **Connection** object.

A good example of when to use a transaction is when you conduct a bulk update operation against a set of records. As you are aware, when you engage in such an operation from the user interface side of Microsoft Access you are prompted with a message that informs you of the number of records you are about to modify and asks permission to continue or lets you abandon the operation. Using a transaction you can elicit the same type of message from within VBA code using either DAO or ADO. Presented below are two code examples that both conduct the same type of transaction-based bulk update. A department name in a table (*tblHRData*) will be changed from the value *IT* to *Information Technology*. A counter (*intCounter*) tracks the number of edits about to be committed and if greater than zero, presents the user with a message box that details the number of records which will be changed. If the user does not select the *Yes* button the transaction is cancelled, otherwise the changes are committed.

**Using Transactions in DAO:**

```vba
Dim wks         As Workspace
Dim db          As Database
Dim rec         As Recordset
Dim intCounter  As Integer
Dim strMsg      As String

Set wks = DBEngine.Workspaces(0)

Set db = CurrentDb
Set rec = db.OpenRecordset("tblHRData")

wks.BeginTrans
    rec.MoveFirst
    Do
        If rec![Department] = "IT" Then
            intCounter = intCounter + 1
            rec.Edit
            rec![Department] = "Information Technology"
            rec.Update
        End If
        rec.MoveNext
    Loop Until rec.EOF

    If intCounter = 0 Then MsgBox "No records affected": Exit
        Sub

    strMsg = intCounter & " records are affected. Continue?"
    If MsgBox(strMsg, vbYesNo, "Edit Records") = vbYes Then
        wks.CommitTrans
    Else
        wks.Rollback
    End If

rec.Close
db.Close
wks.Close
Set rec = Nothing
Set db = Nothing
Set wks = Nothing
```

**Using Transactions in ADO:**

```
Dim cnn        As ADODB.Connection
Dim rec        As ADODB.Recordset
Dim intCounter As Integer
Dim strMsg     As String

Set rec = New ADODB.Recordset

Set cnn = CurrentProject.Connection
rec.Open "tblHRData", cnn, adOpenDynamic, adLockOptimistic

cnn.BeginTrans
rec.MoveFirst
  Do
     If rec![Department] = "IT" Then
        rec.Edit
        intCounter = intCounter + 1
        rec![Department] = "Information Technology"
        rec.Update
     End If
     rec.MoveNext
  Loop Until rec.EOF

  If intCounter=0 Then MsgBox "No records affected": Exit Sub

  strMsg = intCounter & " records are affected. Continue?"
  If MsgBox(strMsg, vbYesNo, "Edit Records") = vbYes Then
     cnn.CommitTrans
  Else
     cnn.RollbackTrans
  End If

rec.Close
cnn.Close
```

 Transactions are useful when you need to conduct an operation on a batch of records where complete consistency is mission critical. Transactions against data managed over a network ensure that the bulk operation either completely succeeds or completely fails.

# Creating a New Table

Data access technologies permit the creation of tables as well as manipulating table data. For DAO this is a native task managed by manipulating a **Database** object and working with the **TableDefs** collection. This approach works both for native Microsoft Access databases as well as ODBC databases (provided your process has sufficient permissions to create tables on a distant server).

In ADO an additional object library is required, the *Microsoft ADO Ext. X.X For DLL and Security* in order to access the **Catalog** object, which is used to manipulate database objects such as tables. The ADOX object model was introduced in Chapter 10.

In the following examples, we present procedures in both technologies for creating a table in the local database. The table includes a primary key field. In DAO this is mediated by manipulating an **Index** object. In ADO primary keys are a natural part of the **Keys** collection of a **Table** object.

Both examples include an error handler that deletes an existing table if one exists with the same name as the newly created table. Be cautious when using this approach in your own code. When a table is deleted programmatically the user will not be alerted and the action is irreversible.

**Using DAO to Create a Table:**

```
Sub DAOCreateTable()
On Error GoTo DAOError

Dim db As Database
Dim tbl As DAO.TableDef
Dim idx As DAO.Index

'establish the db connection
Set db = CurrentDb
Set tbl = db.CreateTableDef("DAO Table Test")
'create the table fields
With tbl
  .Fields.Append .CreateField("PrimaryKey_Field", dbInteger)
  .Fields.Append .CreateField("FirstName", dbText)
  .Fields.Append .CreateField("LastName", dbText)
  .Fields.Append .CreateField("DOB", dbDate)
End With

'append the table to the database
db.TableDefs.Append tbl
db.TableDefs.Refresh

'Create the primary key on the existing table
Set tbl = db.TableDefs("DAO Table Test")
With tbl
  Set idx = .CreateIndex("NewIndex")
  With idx
    .Fields.Append .CreateField("PrimaryKey_Field")
    .Primary = True
  End With
  .Indexes.Append idx
End With
db.TableDefs.Refresh

Exit Sub
DAOError:
  If err.number = 3010 Then
    db.TableDefs.Delete "DAO Table Test"
    Resume
  End If

End Sub
```

**Using ADO to Create a Table:**

```
Sub ADOCreateTable()
Dim Cn      As ADODB.Connection
Dim cat     As ADOX.Catalog
Dim objTable As ADOX.Table
Dim err     As ADODB.Error

On Error GoTo ADOError

  Set Cn = New ADODB.Connection
  Set cat = New ADOX.Catalog
  Set objTable = New ADOX.Table

'Open the connection
  Set Cn = CurrentProject.Connection

'Open the Catalog
  Set cat.ActiveConnection = Cn

'Create the table and append fields and primary key
With objTable
  .Name ="Test_Table"
  .Columns.Append "PrimaryKey_Field", adInteger
  .Columns.Append "FirstName", adVarWChar
  .Columns.Append "LastName", adVarWChar
  .Columns.Append "DOB", adDate
  .Keys.Append "PrimaryKey", adKeyPrimary, _
     "PrimaryKey_Field"
End With

'Append the newly created table to the Tables Collection
  cat.Tables.Append objTable

'clean up objects
  Set objTable = Nothing
  Set cat = Nothing
  Cn.Close
  Set Cn = Nothing
  Exit Sub
```

```
ADOError:
  For Each err In Cn.Errors
    MsgBox err.Description & vbCrLf & err.Number
    If err.Number = -2147217857 Then
      cat.Tables.Delete "Test_Table"
      Resume
    End If
  Next

End Sub
```

 Although the ADO code appears longer (we are manipulating more
objects), conceptually it is a simpler object model. Review the differences
between forming a primary key in the DAO code vs. the ADO code.

# Creating a New Database

Creating a new database using DAO or ADO is similar to creating new tables in that a database
object is native to DAO while a Catalog object in ADO requires that you reference the ADOX
extension library. In DAO, a database is a child of the **Workspace** object. The following DAO
code first tests for the existence of a database named *NewDB .accdb* and if it exists, deletes it before
creating a new database of that name:

```
Dim wksp As Workspace
Dim db As Database
Dim prp As Property

Set wksp = CreateWorkspace("AccessWorkspace", "admin", _
    "", dbUseJet)

' Make sure there isn't already a file with the name of
' the new database.
If Dir("C:\Temp\NewDB.accdb") <> "" Then Kill
    "C:\Temp\NewDB.accdb"

' Create a new database with the specified
' collating order.
Set db = wksp.CreateDatabase("C:\Temp\NewDB.accdb", _
    dbLangGeneral)
db.Close
wksp.Close
```

When you use ADOX to create a Microsoft Access database, you reference the underlying JET (Joint Enhancement Technology) engine that underlies Microsoft Access. This reference is through the Provider argument of the **Create** method of the **Catalog** object. As in the previous example, if a database of the name *new.accdb* exists it is deleted before making a database with that name:

```
Dim cat As New ADOX.Catalog

If Dir("C:\Temp\new.accdb") <> "" Then Kill
    "C:\Temp\new.accdb"
cat.Create "Provider= Microsoft.ACE.OLEDB.12.0;Data
    Source=c:\Temp\new.accdb"

Set cat = Nothing
```

# DAO/ADO Examples

We will focus on a few examples that highlight the power of working with DAO and ADO. In one case, we will revisit the table of contents example that was discussed on page 143. Other examples record the results of edits made to financial data, clean up data for import, and migrate data from Access to MySQL.

## Using DAO to Create a Table of Contents

This subject was first visited in Chapter 8. It uses the **Print** event of either a report **Detail** or a **GroupHeader** section to populate a table with information that ultimately feeds to a second report to generate a table of contents for the primary report. The appeal of that approach is that working with the **DoCMD** object required code in only two places, the report **Open** event to delete the contents of the tblTOC table (used to store data for a table of contents report) and some code in the appropriate report section to actually populate the tblTOC table.

The DAO approach requires a bit more code but conceptually is a cleaner approach (for example, we don't need to evoke the **SetWarnings** method to toggle warning messages). Briefly, code is required in the following locations:

- The **General Declaration** section of the module for the report is used to declare a recordset object. Recall that placing declarative code in this section raises the scope and lifetime of a variable to the entire report module.

- The report's **Open** event contains code to empty the contents of the tblTOC table, as well as opening the recordset object.

- The **Print** event for a **Detail** or **GroupHeader** section (in this example we'll use the latter) contains code that populates the tblTOC table.
- The report's **Close** event closes and deinstantiates the recordset object.

The combined code for a report named *Department_Project_Budget* appears below:

```
'General Declarations section:
Dim rec As DAO.Recordset

Private Sub Report_Open(Cancel As Integer)

'first delete records in the current tblTOC table
CurrentDb.Execute "DELETE * FROM tblTOC;"

Set rec = CurrentDb.OpenRecordset("tblTOC", dbOpenTable, _
        dbAppendOnly, dbOptimistic)

End Sub

Private Sub Report_Close()

rec.Close
Set rec = Nothing

End Sub

'the Group Header Code:
Private Sub GroupHeader0_Print(Cancel As Integer, PrintCount _
        As Integer)

'populate table with new data
With rec
    .AddNew
    ![Entry] = Me.Department
    ![PageNumber] = Me.Page
    .Update
End With

End Sub
```

## Using DAO to Log Transactions

A common feature of databases that manage financial information is a transaction log. This is a table that stores information about every change to a financial record and can be used to track changes, audit records, or rebuild a table following a significant failure. In this example we will log changes to a table that stores project budget information. A transaction table, named *tblTransactionLog* stores information about every change to budget information, including the addition of new records. The majority of the code is located in the form's **BeforeUpdate** event. However, deleting a record skips that event so a parallel section of code occurs in the **Delete** event for the form. Like the previous example, the recordset is declared in the form module's **General Declarations** section, and the recordset is instantiated and opened in the form's **Open** event, and closed and deinstantiated in the form's **Close** event.

The code required appears below:

```
'General Declarations section:
Dim rec As DAO.Recordset


Private Sub Form_Open(Cancel As Integer)
'establish a connection when the form opens. Close it when the
      form is closed
Set rec = CurrentDb.OpenRecordset("tblTransactionLog",
      dbOpenTable, dbAppendOnly, dbOptimistic)
End Sub


Private Sub Form_BeforeUpdate(Cancel As Integer)
'record edits to the project budget information
   With rec
    .AddNew
    ![User] = Application.CurrentUser
    ![Project] = Me.Parent.ProjectName.Value
    ![StaffName] = Me.cboStaffName.Column(1) & _
          " " & Me.cboStaffName.Column(2)
    ![OldValue] = Me.Budget.OldValue
    ![NewValue] = Me.Budget.Value
    ![EditTimeStamp] = Now()
    If IsNull(Me.Budget.OldValue) Then
        ![Action] = "ADD"
    Else
        ![Action] = "EDIT"
    End If
    .Update
   End With
End Sub
```

```
Private Sub Form_Delete(Cancel As Integer)
    With rec
        .AddNew
        ![User] = Application.CurrentUser
        ![Project] = Me.Parent.ProjectName.Value
        ![StaffName] = Me.cboStaffName.Column(1) & " " &
          Me.cboStaffName.Column(2)
        ![OldValue] = Me.Budget.OldValue
        ![NewValue] = Me.Budget.Value
        ![EditTimeStamp] = Now()
        ![Action] = "DELETED"
        .Update
    End With
End Sub


Private Sub Form_Close()
    rec.Close
    Set rec = Nothing
End Sub
```

An example of such a transaction log is illustrated below.

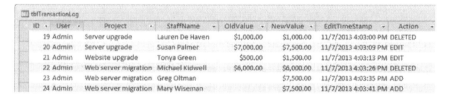

## Using DAO to Clean Imported Data

Cleaning data for import is a common use of either DAO or ADO. In this example, based
roughly on scores of real-world examples, we'll assume that a table exists in Access that contains
data which violate several rules of database normalization. An example of such a table is illustrated
below.

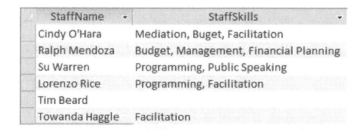

The first violation of normalization occurs in the *StaffName* field. The full staff name is being used, rather than dedicating a field for first and last name (try to sort on last name using this table!). The second violation occurs with the list of staff skills. Ideally these should be broken into another table and associated with each staff member using a primary key-foreign key pair.

Fixing this data requires two tables. One to store the staff name (along with a primary key). The second table will contain a foreign key field to relate skills back to each staff member, and a field that will house individual skills. Thus in the example above, Cindy O'Hara will have three records in the foreign key table—one record of each of the three skills associated with her. Towanda Haggle will have a single record in that table, while Tim Beard will not have a record in the skills table.

In the nutshell, this is the procedure:

Step 1.    Establish three **Recordset** variables. One to read data from the table containing the "bad" data (tblExport). Another recordset will write basic staff information and generate a primary key in a new table (tblImportStaff) while a third recordset writes skills, along with a foreign key value into a second new table (tblImportSkill). Also establish the various variables to assist in storing staff first and last names, an array of skills, and the newly-generated primary key.

Step 2.    Instantiate the three recordset objects.

Step 3.    Begin a loop to cycle through each record in the bad data—this is table tblExport.

Step 4.    For each staff record, break the value in the *StaffName* field into two pieces. We'll use the **Split()** function which accepts a string to split as the first argument and the delimiter, or what is used to denote where to split, as the second argument. **Split()** returns an Array of the **String** data type.

Step 5.    Populate the *FirstName* and *LastName* fields in the tblImportStaff table. Update the table and get the newly generated primary key. We'll use the SELECT @@IDENTITY SQL statement to obtain the primary key. This command is recognized by many major databases, including Microsoft SQL Server, MySQL, and Access.

Step 6.    If the current staff member has one or more skills listed, step into a loop to **Split()** those skills—here we'll use a **For..Each** loop to get each individual skill (the variable must be of the **Variant** data type when working with **For..Each**). Within this loop we load records into the second new table, tblImportSkills. The two fields loaded are the current primary key value (obtained in Step 5), and one of the skills listed for the current staff member. This process cycles until all listed skills have been processed.

Step 7.  Return to the main loop and cycle to the next staff member listed in the tblExport table. Once all staff have been processed, close each of the three recordsets.

The code for this process appears below:

```
Dim recImport  As DAO.Recordset
Dim recPKtbl   As DAO.Recordset
Dim recFKtbl   As DAO.Recordset
Dim varPK      As Variant 'for primary key
Dim strName()    As String 'for array of name pairs
Dim strSkills() As String 'array of skills
Dim varSkill     As Variant 'individual skill in For..Each


Set recImport = CurrentDb.OpenRecordset("tblExport")
Set recPKtbl = CurrentDb.OpenRecordset("tblImportStaff")
Set recFKtbl = CurrentDb.OpenRecordset("tblImportSkill")
```

```
'cycle through export table and extract names
recImport.MoveFirst
Do
    'populate main table with atomic names
    With recPKtbl
        .AddNew
        strName = Split(recImport![StaffName], " ")
        ![FirstName] = strName(0)  'first name
        ![LastName] = strName(1)  'last name
        .Update
    End With
    'get primary key then reopen tblImportStaff
    recPKtbl.Close
    Set recPKtbl = CurrentDb.OpenRecordset("SELECT
      @@IDENTITY")
    varPK = recPKtbl.Fields(0) 'IDENTITY returns 1 value
    recPKtbl.Close
    Set recPKtbl = CurrentDb.OpenRecordset("tblImportStaff")
    'now populate foreign key table
    If recImport![StaffSkills] <> "" Then 'skip empties
        strSkills() = Split(recImport![StaffSkills], ",")
        For Each varSkill In strSkills
            With recFKtbl
                .AddNew
                ![FK] = varPK
                ![StaffSkill] = varSkill
                .Update
            End With
        Next
    End If
    'move to the next record in tblExport
    recImport.MoveNext
Loop Until recImport.EOF
'close the recordsets
recImport.Close
recPKtbl.Close
recFKtbl.Close

End Sub
```

If data from the table illustrated on page 196 were run through this code two tables would be populated with data. Table tblImportStaff would appear as:

| SID ▾ | FirstName ▾ | LastName ▾ |
|---|---|---|
| 14 | Cindy | O'Hara |
| 15 | Ralph | Mendoza |
| 16 | Su | Warren |
| 17 | Lorenzo | Rice |
| 18 | Tim | Beard |
| 19 | Towanda | Haggle |

While the foreign key table, tblImportSkills would appear as:

| FK ▾ | StaffSkill ▾ |
|---|---|
| 14 | Buget |
| 14 | Facilitation |
| 14 | Mediation |
| 15 | Financial Planning |
| 15 | Management |
| 15 | Budget |
| 16 | Public Speaking |
| 16 | Programming |
| 17 | Facilitation |
| 17 | Programming |
| 19 | Facilitation |

This example presents a cleaner set of data than is typically encountered by most programmers charged with importing data from another source into an Access database. Still, beyond some manual cleaning that may be required, using DAO to migrate thousands of records saves many hours of tedious work. Imagine manually breaking the original data set into two related tables!

## Using ADO and DAO to Migrate Data

In this last example we'll bring ADO into the code in order to efficiency manage a recordset from a production server. The native Access data will be managed via DAO. An example of migrating data may be to securely archive important data stored in Access, or to conduct some sort of migration to a server that makes the data available to some web server. In the code example, we are assuming that there are tables on both servers of the same structure. The table in Access is named tblHRData and a complimentary table is located on a MySQL server, here accessed through a DSN connection named *MySQL_Ubuntu*. The complimentary table is named tblHRData_Archive. The code is fairly straightforward:

```vba
Sub C11_ExportData()

Dim recAccess As DAO.Recordset

Dim cnnMySQL As ADODB.Connection
Dim recMySQL As ADODB.Recordset

'establish the Access connection
Set recAccess = CurrentDb.OpenRecordset("tblHRData")

'establish the MySQL connection
Set cnnMySQL = New ADODB.Connection
Set recMySQL = New ADODB.Recordset
cnnMySQL.Open ("DSN=MySQL_Ubuntu")
recMySQL.Open "tblHRData_Archive", cnnMySQL, adOpenDynamic, _
        adLockOptimistic


'cycle through the records in access
recAccess.MoveFirst
Do
    'populate records in the MySQL recordset
    recMySQL.AddNew
    recMySQL![ID] = recAccess![ID]
    recMySQL![FirstName] = recAccess![FirstName]
    recMySQL![LastName] = recAccess![LastName]
    recMySQL![Department] = recAccess![Department]
    recMySQL![JobTitle] = recAccess![JobTitle]
    recMySQL![StartDate] = recAccess![StartDate]
    recMySQL![EndDate] = recAccess![EndDate]
    recMySQL.Update

    recAccess.MoveNext

Loop Until recAccess.EOF

recAccess.Close
recMySQL.Close

End Sub
```

# Chapter 12 | Automation Programming

Automation involves using VBA to manipulate the object model of another application. The specific technology is called COM, which Microsoft defines as Component Object Model. When you manipulate the object model in Access, or use DAO or ADO for data access, you are working with COM objects. Automation extends that functionality to the other members of the Microsoft Office suite, many of the elements of the Windows operating system, and hundreds of other applications that run on Windows.

COM is a powerful technology. For example, much of what you can do from within Microsoft Excel may be accessed in Access via COM and VBA code. One of the examples we will step through proves this point by using Excel to calculate the depreciation for an asset given some assumptions. Excel ships with a wider array of built-in formulas for such financial operations than Access. COM permits you to stitch these two applications together.

There are three considerations you should be mindful of when working with COM:

- COM requires that library references be set to the desired object library. Just like when working with DAO and ADO.

- When you evoke an application object such as Microsoft Excel you are actually loading an instance of Excel into memory. The object may not be visible to you or your end users but COM does consume system resources.

- Related to the second point, sloppy programming can lead to multiple instances of an application all running and therefore consuming memory. Especially during development, if your computer seems to suddenly slow down, check **Task Manager** to ensure that you haven't set up multiple copies of the object you are attempting to work with.

The most important point about COM is that the successful programmer should understand the object model of the application being evoked. Like DAO and ADO, you must frequently step through an object hierarchy in order to manipulate the target object. For example, in Microsoft Excel each cell within a worksheet is a **Range** object. A user of Excel has at a minimum an intuitive understanding that cells are owned by worksheets which are owned by workbooks. The workbook object is a child of the application object (which maps to Excel itself). Knowledge of an application's object model helps when you use COM to automate some aspect of the application. In this case you know that to manipulate a **Range** object in Excel, you also need to evoke a

**Workbook** object, and depending upon the task at hand, a **Worksheet** object may be required as well.

## Library References

In the same manner in which you first establish library references when working with DAO or ADO, you must first set appropriate object library references before you can begin coding a COM object. Setting a library reference exposes the target application's objects, their properties, and methods to your current application. Once a library reference is set, you'll notice when coding that the autolist members and autolist for properties and methods feature will recognize the object keywords for the remote application.

Setting a library reference was discussed on page 163.

## Early vs. Late Binding

When you use declarative statements to specifically define the objects you will be working with, you are using early binding. An early binding to an Excel worksheet from within Access would take the form:

```
Dim wks As Excel.Worksheet
'more code
Set wks = Excel.Workbooks.Open("R:\Sample.xls")
```

An alternative approach is to vaguely reference an object and then, at the last minute, specifically reference the object to a particular object type. This approach is called late binding and would appear as:

```
Dim wks As Object
'more code
Set wks = CreateObject("Excel.Worksheet")
```

Late binding was the original programming method used in automation and its inclusion in modern programming languages is for backward compatibility. Refrain from using it as the approach requires more resources and is much slower than early binding.

 Avoid using the **New** keyword when declaring an object variable because it instantiates the object immediately. You have more control over your object if you declare it without the **New** keyword, and use the **Set** keyword to instantiate the object when you need it.

## Controlling Memory Leaks

When using COM there is a great potential for spawning processes that continue to use memory and system resources even after your code has stopped running. Unlike Java, VB and VBA do not automatically scan for these memory leaks in your application. It is your responsibility to ensure that resources are released once you are finished working with an automation object. The guidelines are straightforward:

- When you are finished with an automation object that is not an application, release its resources by setting the object to Nothing.

- When working with an application object, first use the application's Quit method, then set its reference to Nothing.

The code fragment below illustrates these methods:

```
'This is an Application object
Dim appObj As Excel.Application
'This is an Excel object
Dim wks as Excel.Worksheet
'lots of code
'When done, release the objects resources
'first the Excel Object
Set wks = Nothing
'Now the application object
appObj.Quit
Set appObj = Nothing
```

## Creating the Object Reference

The procedure for creating an early-binding object reference is outlined below:

Step 1.     From a code window, set the appropriate object library reference. Refer to the procedure on page 163 for details.

Step 2.     Use declarative statements to create the object variables you will need.

Step 3.     Instantiate each object reference by using the **Set** statement.

Step 4.     After each object's useful period has ended, and before the scope and lifetime of the code are extinguished, remember to set each object reference to **Nothing** (*deinstantiate* the object). If an object refers to an *Application*, first use the application's **Quit** method.

## Additional Points on Automation

Automation is a powerful technique but there are pitfalls that must be considered. Some of the most important points concerning automation are listed below.

- Calling an incorrect method or referring to an incorrect property of an automation object may sometimes cause Windows to freeze up. When writing and testing code you may need to save your work frequently to avoid loss.

- Some methods applied to an automation object may cause the object to respond with a message box or some other system call. If the automation object is not visible, as is the case if you are working with an application object with its **Visible** property set to false, then the application will appear to be frozen as it awaits input from the user. To avoid this situation you need to anticipate such conditions and ensure that your code does not raise them. Note that this condition may also arise when working with automation objects owned by an application. An example is evoking a hidden worksheet, changing its data, and attempting to close the object. Excel will respond with the message box, "*Save changes?*

- Within the Office suite, only Outlook and PowerPoint support m*ultiple use* modes. All other applications within the suite are *single use*. Whenever your code automates a *single use* application another instance of the application is created. When referring to a *multiple use* application that is already running no new instance is created.

As already discussed, you need to remember to destroy all object references once your code is finished with them. For applications, use the **Quit** method before setting the object to *Nothing*.

# Using COM to Provide Additional Functionality

Most developers use COM to conduct some operation which is not available to them from the immediate coding environment. In this section we will examine three such examples. In the first the Excel object model is used from within Access to conduct a financial calculation. The second example shows how to automate Excel to pull data in from an Access database. This type of operation is also available from the Excel user interface but in this example the code can be attached to some event such as a command button or the **Open** event of a **Workbook** object. The final example outlines how to program **Internet Explorer** from within Access. The example shows how to download the **InnerHTML** property of a **Document** object. Although this code example is relatively trivial, with a bit of imagination one could build a scanning routine that monitors certain web content and alerts the user when a page changes, or an archival utility that stores the content of a website that changes frequently.

## Using an Excel Function in Access

In the introduction to this Chapter it was mentioned that Excel provides formula functions that are not available in Access. One example is the function to calculate amount an asset depreciates for each accounting period based on some assumptions. The **AMORLINC** function in Excel takes the form:

```
AMORLINC(cost, date_purchased, first_period, salvage, period, rate,
      basis)
```

| Argument | Description |
|---|---|
| Cost | The initial cost of the asset. |
| Date purchased | The purchase date, entered using the DATE() function. Thus, for an asset purchased on 1 July 2010 you would use DATE(2010, 07, 01) |
| First period | The date of the first accounting period. For example, a fiscal year ending 31 Dec 2010 would appear as DATE(2010, 12, 31). |
| Salvage | The salvage value at the end of the asset's useful life. |
| Period | An argument that sets whether payments are made at the beginning of the payment period (here in *Months* or at the end. The default is *0* meaning that payment is expected at the end of the month. You would use *1* to specify that payment is due at the beginning of the month. |
| Rate | The rate of depreciation (straight-line depreciation is assumed for this function). |
| Basis | The year basis. The function expects 0 for 360 days (NASD method), 1 for Actual, 2 for 365 days, and 4 for 360 days using the European method. |

To calculate the yearly depreciation on an asset purchased for $100,000 in July 2010, with an accounting period that ends on 31 December 2010, a salvage cost of $25,000, and assuming a 10% depreciation rate, in Excel you would enter the following formula in a cell of a worksheet:

```
=AMORLINC(100000,DATE(2010, 7, 1),DATE(2010, 12,
      31),25000,1,10%,1)
```

Excel would return **10,000** which represents the amount the asset would depreciate each year. Clearly this isn't a function available to Access unless you evoke COM. The following code, contained within a code module in Microsoft Access, conducts this same calculation and dumps the formula output to the debug window. A library reference to the **Microsoft Excel Object Library** was set prior to writing the code. With a little reengineering and knowledge of DAO or ADO it's pretty easy to extend this example to one that would populate field values in a table instead.

```
Sub ExcelAutomation()
Dim app     As Excel.Application
Dim wkb     As Excel.Workbook

  Set app = New Excel.Application
  Set wkb = app.Workbooks.Add

  wkb.Worksheets("Sheet1").Activate
  Activecell.Formula = "=AMORLINC(100000,DATE(2010, 7,
      1),DATE(2010, 12, 31),25000,1,10%,1)"
  Debug.Print ActiveCell.Value

  app.Quit
  Set app = Nothing
  Set wkb = Nothing

End Sub
```

Similar to working with DAO or ADO, there are usually several ways to code for the same results. In this case the developer is using a built-in shortcut in Excel named **ActiveCell** that refers to the worksheet cell that currently has the focus. In a new worksheet this is always cell A1. Another way to code that line would be: ActiveSheet.Range("A1").Formula=.... or Worksheets("Sheet1").Range("A1").Formula=...

## Copying Access Data into Excel

When working in another application, such as Excel, you do not need to set an object reference to the Access application to manipulate Access data via ADO/ADOX. You must, however, set a library reference to the appropriate ADO libraries.

The following code, run from within a general module in Microsoft Excel, opens a table (*tblPopulation*) in an Access database and copies the contents of the table's three fields (*Rank*, *State*, and *Population*) into the first two columns of the current worksheet.

```
Sub CopyAccessData_to_Excel()
Dim cnnDb  As ADODB.Connection
Dim rec    As ADODB.Recordset
Dim rng    As Excel.Range
```

```vba
' Use connection to a remote Access database
Set cnnDb = New ADODB.Connection
cnnDb.Provider = "Microsoft.ACE.OLEDB.12.0"
cnnDb.Open "C:\Temp\access data.accdb"
Set rec = New ADODB.Recordset
rec.Open "tblPopulation", cnnDb, adOpenKeyset,
        adLockOptimistic


rec.MoveFirst

'establish a pointer to cell A1
Set rng = ActiveSheet.Range("A1")
rng.Activate

Do
 rng.Value = rec![Rank]
 ActiveCell.Offset(0, 1).Value = rec![State]
 ActiveCell.Offset(0, 2).Value = rec![Population]
 ActiveCell.Offset(1, 0).Select 'offset the pointer one
 Set rng = ActiveCell             'row down and over.
 rec.MoveNext
Loop While Not rec.EOF


'clear all object references
Set rng = Nothing
Set rec = Nothing
Set cnnDb = Nothing

End Sub
```

 Although the topic of VBA programming from within Microsoft Excel is beyond the scope of this book, the VBA editor is the same in all members of the Microsoft Office Suite. When working with VBA from another Office Suite member, only the member's object model is different.

## Using Internet Explorer to Programmatically Obtain HTML

In this last example we turn to a component of the Windows operating system—Microsoft Internet Explorer. The component necessary to download web content is located in the **Microsoft Internet Controls** library and we will utilize a single **InternetExplorer** object. This object resolves to the Internet Explorer application and can be programmatically manipulated.

The code takes advantage of the fact that most Internet browsers, including Internet Explorer, recognize the Document Object Model (DOM) of HTML documents. When we instruct Internet Explorer to download a web page the code will dump the contents of the **InnerHTML** property into the **Immediate Window**.

```
Sub browser()
Dim ie As InternetExplorer

Set ie = New InternetExplorer
ie.Navigate ("http://www.example.com")

Do While ie.ReadyState <> READYSTATE_COMPLETE
  DoEvents
Loop

Debug.Print ie.Document.body.innerhtml

ie.Quit
Set ie = Nothing

End Sub
```

 If you wish to only access the contents of a web page's **Head** section, the syntax would become Debug.Print ie.Document.head.innerhtml. To access everything between the <HTML> and </HTML> tags the syntax is Debug.Print ie.Document.DocumentElement.innerhtml

The **Do..Loop** serves to prevent VBA from locking up in the event it takes a long time for Internet Explorer to locate and connect to the referenced web page. The **ReadyState** property of the browser returns the intrinsic constant **READYSTATE_COMPLETE** once the requested page is fully downloaded. The **DoEvents** function passes control to the operating system whenever called, thus preventing VBA from freezing under some circumstances.

# Chapter 13 | Developing for Multiple Users

Many Access database applications are constructed for use in a multiuser environment. As a developer of a such a database application you need to consider how this environment will affect your application. In general, the considerations fall into two categories: maintainability and network issues.

## Maintainability

Ideally, you should be able to distribute your application to your users and expect that every copy remains identical, at least in terms of the user interface elements. To maintain control over your application once distributed, you can use the following techniques:

- **Hide some or all of your database objects.** In Access you may hide anything that is normally listed in the Navigation Pane. For many users this technique will effectively prevent them from renaming or deleting your objects.

- **Password protect the entire database**. This gives you some control over those individuals who may work with the database.

- **Password and view-protect your VBA code**. Once protected, the VBA editor cannot be accessed without first entering the password. This protects all code behind forms, reports, and within a general or class module.

- **Distribute your database as an** *accde* **file**. In this form, your database's forms, reports, and modules will not be available in design view. If your database project contains VBA code it only exists within the **accde** file in a complied format and thus cannot be viewed or edited.

- **Distribute your database as a distributable Package** that contains a **Digital Signature**. The package is located on a network resource that your users can access. When they open the package they must save the packaged database to another name.

Regardless of which scheme you adopt, an obvious point is that you must take care to manage version control on your end. Once you ship copies of your database application to other users, version control becomes a serious issue that can trip up developers. Many developers keep a separate folder (here, we will refer to it as FINAL) that only contains the most recent version of a database file for each project. When a bug has been discovered or an additional feature requested, a copy of that file is made and deposited into a development folder where the required work is conducted. Following testing and before deployment, the copy in the FINAL folder is overwritten and the file is redistributed to end users. When working with a split database (discussed beginning on page 226), the *front-end* file is the file that typically sees continued development work while the *back-end* file isn't usually further modified as it contains the database tables and hence the production data.

Another method for controlling access to your database objects, *Users and Groups*, was removed in Access 2010. If you need to preserve the integrity of table and/or query structure, user and group access can be applied at the level of many ODBC-compliant database applications such as Microsoft SQL server or MySQL and by using ADO or DAO you can still elicit some user and group management of those objects.

## How to Hide Database Objects

Hiding a database object simply removes its reference from the **Navigation Pane**. The hidden objects can still be called from other components of your database application. A savvy user can defeat this feature but for general database users this is a simple technique for obfuscating your database. This technique is not mutually exclusive of the other techniques and it a good first start step toward protecting your final design.

Step 1.    For each object you wish to make hidden, first select it from the **Navigation Pane**.

Step 2.    Right-click on the object and select **View Properties** (depending upon the object this option may read **Table** or **Object Properties**) from the shortcut menu.

Step 3.    Check the **Hidden** attribute check box.

You will need to close and reopen the database for this change to take effect.

## How to Unhide Database Objects

You should use the first 4 steps of this procedure during development so you can still see hidden objects. In this mode a hidden object appears in the **Navigation Pane** as a grayed image.

Step 1.    From the **File** menu, choose **Options**.

Step 2.    Select the **Current Database** entry from the left-hand pane.

Step 3.    Move to the **Navigation** section and select the **Navigation Options**.

Step 4.    In the **Display** area, check **Show Hidden Objects**, then choose **OK**.

Step 5.    To continue to unhide an object, return to the **Navigation Pane**. Hidden objects will appear gray. Right-click on the desired object and select **View Properties** from the shortcut menu.

Step 6.    Uncheck the **Hidden** checkbox and choose **OK**.

## Password Protect Your Database

This option by itself only controls who can access the database. Once successfully opened the user has full access to all objects and data within the database. In Access 2007 and later, password protecting a database file also encrypts the file. The topic was not covered in Chapter 11 but if you use DAO or ADO to access a password protected Access database, you must include the password as a value of the **Password** argument in a **OpenDatabase** method in DAO or when using the **Open** method of a **Connection** object in ADO.

 *Warning*: **DO NOT** lose your password if you protect an Access database. The new encrypted format means that forgetting a password effectively renders the database permanently useless.

A database **must** be open in **Exclusive Mode** before applying a password.

Step 1.    If the database is open, close it before proceeding.

Step 2.    From Access, select the **File** menu and then choose **Open** (you cannot open a database in exclusive mode by choosing it from the list of recently-opened files).

Step 3.    Navigate as usual to locate and open the desired database file.

Step 4.    On the **Open** dialog, select the **Open** drop down box and choose **Open Exclusive**.

Step 5.    Once the file has been opened, from the **File** menu, choose **Encrypt with Password**.

Step 6.    In the **Set Password** dialog box, enter the password twice and then choose **OK**.

A password-protected database can be opened by multiple users, as long as no one opens it in exclusive mode. Each person accessing the database must know the password to open the file.

## Removing Password Protection From a Database

The database must be opened in **Exclusive Mode** before removing a password. When you remove a password you also decrypt the database file.

Step 1.     Repeat Steps 1 through 4 from the previous procedure to open the database file.

Step 2.     From the **File** menu, choose **Decrypt Database**.

Step 3.     Enter the database password.

Step 4.     Save the database file.

# Password Protecting VBA Code

You can protect all your VBA code by issuing a password from within the VBA Editor. Protected code may not be viewed unless the correct password is issued. The code behind forms and reports may not be viewed unless the correct password has been entered in the VBA editor.

## How to Password Protect Your Code

Step 1.     Open the VBA Editor.

Step 2.     Select the current project in the **Project Explorer** and right-click on it.

Step 3.     From the shortcut menu, choose *projectname* **Properties.**

Step 4.     On the **Project Properties** dialog box, select the **Protection** tab.

Step 5.     Check the **Lock project for viewing** checkbox to prevent users from viewing your code.

Step 6.     Type a password in the **Password** text box, then type the password again in the **Confirm Password** text box.

Step 7.     Choose **OK.**

To remove the password, first open the database, then open the VBA Editor. Enter the password you created in Step 6. Repeat Steps 2 through 4. Clear the checkmark in the **Lock project for viewing** checkbox, then clear both password text boxes. Choose **OK** when done.

If you are only working with a single project, you may also jump to Step 3 above by choosing *projectname* **Properties** from the **Tools** menu.

# Making an ACCDE File

An Access database file with the *accde* extension is essentially a locked down version of a standard accdb file. The basic difference is that *no one* can edit existing forms, reports, macros or modules, create such objects, or modify or create VBA code. Users may still create and modify tables and queries in an accde file.

You must take care to safely maintain a working copy of the database from which the accde file was derived. This is because you cannot work on an accde file once it is created. All changes and updates to the user interface elements must be done with the accdb version. If you need to make changes to a distributed accde file you must make the changes in the original accdb file and recreate the accde version.

## How to Create an accde File

Access makes a copy of the original file in order to create an accde file. The original database file is not altered during this process but you should take care to preserve the original file. If you lose the file that an accde file was created from you lose the ability to modify most of the user interface elements.

Step 1.     From the **Tools** menu, choose **Save & Publish.**

Step 2.     In the **Database File Types** area, select **Make ACCDE**, then select **Save As.**

Step 3.     Save the new file to the desired location and file name. When the process is complete you will be returned to the original Access database file.

## Opening an accde File

When you open an unsigned accde file, Access warns you that the content may not be trusted. If you trust the originator of the file, choose **Open**. If you are unsure, **Cancel** the process. Creating a **Trusted Location** to place your shared database files is discussed later in this Chapter. Any Access database file placed in such a location will open without any warnings.

# Package and Sign a Database File

This approach requires that you have a *digital certificate* to attach to your database file. Certificates are either purchased by third-party vendors who vet your credentials as a trusted individual or vendor (there are costs associated with this approach), by your organization using Microsoft Certificate Server, or generated by yourself. If your intent is to develop for a smaller group of clients or within a workgroup, you can create a self-signed certificate using the **SelfCert.exe** application that ships with the Microsoft Office suite. Using **SelfCert.exe** is discussed below.

## How to Create a Self-Signed Digital Certificate

Use this technique if you are creating a certificate for your own use or for use by a small group of co-workers or clients. If **SelfCert.exe** is not located on your computer it can be downloaded from the Microsoft website.

Step 1.    Locate the executable file **SELFCERT.exe** using My Computer or Windows Explorer. It is usually located in the root of the current **Microsoft Office** folder.

Step 2.    Run **SELFCERT.exe**

Step 3.    Provide a name for your certificate, then choose OK. Windows will create the certificate and place it in a location reserved for certificates.

## How to Package and Sign a Database

When you follow this procedure, Access creates a copy of your original database file to make the package file. The package file will have an *accdc* file extension. When an end user selects this package, the original file is opened and they are prompted to save the database file locally. The packaged file remains unaltered during this process and unpackaged file will retain the original *accdb* file extension. Packaging and signing a database file only certifies to your end users that the database contains a digital certificate. It does not protect your objects or VBA code from modification. Follow the other procedures in this Chapter such as password protecting your VBA code if such protection is desired.

Step 1.  Open the database file you wish to package and sign. From the **File** menu choose **Save & Publish**.

Step 2.  In the **Save Database As** area, select **Package and Sign**, then choose **Save As.**

Step 3.  In the **Confirm Certificate** dialog box, select the desired certificate (if there are more than one), then choose **OK**.

Step 4.  Select the desired storage location and name for the packaged database. When Access has created the packaged and signed file you are returned to the original database file.

## Opening a Packaged and Signed Database

Step 1.  Locate the package file and open it.

Step 2.  If the certificate isn't fully trusted, Access will warn you. Choose to open the package anyway (**OK**) or abort the process by choosing **Cancel**.

Step 3.  Select a location and file name for the unpackaged file. Choose **OK** when done.

Step 4.  Use the file as you would any other Access database file. The package file remains unaltered during this process.

# Working with Trusted Locations

Another approach to creating trusted database files is to use a trusted file location. Files such as an Access Database which may contain potentially dangerous content such as a macro of VBA code will not be analyzed by the **Trust Center** when stored in a **Trusted Folder**. If you are part of a larger organization your network administrator may have created such folders on your network. If you are developing for a smaller group of workers you can create a trusted folder on your own. Any Access database placed within a trusted folder will be trusted when opened. Indeed, any Microsoft Office file that contains potentially dangerous code will be trusted as long as the file originates from a trusted folder location.

## How to Create a Trusted Location Folder

You should follow this procedure if you are the administrator for a small network. In larger organizations the system administrator typically conducts this task:

Step 1.    From within Microsoft Access, select the **File** menu, then choose **Options**.

Step 2.    Select **Trust Center** from the left hand pane.

Step 3.    In the **Microsoft Trust Center** area, select **Trust Center Settings…**

Step 4.    Select **Trusted Locations** from the left hand pane.

Step 5.    If you need to add a network location, ensure that the **Allow Trusted Locations on my network** checkbox is checked.

Step 6.    Select **Add new location…**

Step 7.    On the **Microsoft Office Trusted Location** dialog box, choose **Browse**, then navigate to the desired folder and select it. You will return to the **Microsoft Office Trusted Location** dialog box.

Step 8.    If you wish to mark subfolders of the selected folder as trusted, check the **Subfolders of this location are also trusted** checkbox. Optionally, enter some descriptive text in the **Description** area.

Step 9.    Choose **OK** when done.

# Network Considerations

Beyond concerns for maintaining and preserving your database's objects, the developer must also be concerned with the act of accessing data in a networked environment. There are two basic network considerations: network traffic and record locking.

## Network Options

The following outlines the various methods you can use to share an Access database over a network:

- **File Sharing — Entire Database**. This scheme involves moving the Access database to a shared folder on a network drive. By default, Access databases are opened in shared mode. Multiple users can access the data concurrently, but every database operation involves moving all the related objects and data across the network. Additionally, because there is only one copy of the database file, you cannot develop separate solutions for subsets of users of the data. Of the multiuser options this one is the least preferable.

- **File Sharing — Split Database**. In this scheme, only the database tables are moved to a shared network folder. Each client workstation maintains a separate copy of the database, but without the tables. Because the forms, reports and other non-table database objects are local, network traffic is reduced. Further, you can develop separate versions of the database to support specific needs of subgroups of users. For applications using relatively few users or where concurrency of data is not an important issue, this option is the preferred choice. The topic of working with a split database is discussed on page 226.

- **Client Server**. This is an advanced solution that involves using Access databases to work with the data, but the data itself is stored in a client-server database such as Microsoft SQL Server or MySQL. Network traffic is greatly reduced in this scheme. However, a drawback is that you have little or no control over the data itself unless you also serve the role as the database administrator on the server side. That said, for high traffic environments and/or where concurrency is an important issue, this is the preferred choice.

## Record Locking

Record locking is required to handle those situations when there are multiple, simultaneous edits to a single record. Most database applications handle this situation by permitting the developer to define the specific access rights to a particular record (this issue arose as properties of either the **OpenDatabase** method of the DAO **Database** object, or the **Open** method of the **Connection** object in ADO). The access rights used by Access are:

- **No Locks**. With this option, the second person attempting to edit the same record is given three choices: overwrite the first person's edits, copy the current edits to the clipboard, or abandon the current edits. All records may always be edited but conflicts between the most recent version of a record's data may occur when more than one person is working on the same data. This is the default locking option.

- **All Records**. This is the most restrictive locking option. All records from all accessed tables are locked while the first person edits any record in the record set. All persons are prevented from editing any records in the locked table(s) until the first person completes his or her editing actions. This option, because of its severe restrictions, is rarely used.

- **Edited Record**. In this option Access locks the records being used by the first person to access them. Anyone attempting to edit the locked records is prevented from doing so until they are released. Everyone may read a locked record. This option ensures that users are viewing only one copy of the data from any given record.

In addition, you can control whether individual records or *pages* are locked. Although page locking may improve your database's performance somewhat, a page is roughly 4K bytes of database data. Thus, if your individual records are small, say 100 bytes, Access will lock some 40 records (4000/100) rather than locking only the record being edited.

### How to Specify Record Locking Options

Step 1.        From the **File** menu, choose **Options**.

Step 2.        From the left-hand pane choose **Client Settings**.

Step 3.        Move to the **Advanced** area and choose the desired option using the following table as a guide:

| Option | Description |
| --- | --- |
| **No Locking** | Few users or infrequent use of the data. |
| **Edited Record** | Many users or frequent use of the data. |
| **All Records** | Few users and mission critical data. |
| **Open databases by using record-level locking** | Specifies record-level or page-level locking. The default is record-level which gives the best performance. |

Step 4.        Choose **OK**

The record or page-level locking scheme will apply to the database only when it is opened next and then only when it is opened by using the **Open** command on the **File** menu.

# Working with a Split Database

Splitting a database into two files, one containing the tables and the other containing all other objects, is a useful technique to improve database performance in a multiuser environment. With a split database there is a single file containing the data and any number of files containing the user interface objects such as queries, forms, and reports. The file containing the tables is referred to as the *back-end* file. The user interface files are referred to as the *front-end* files. Each front-end file contains symbolic links to the tables in the back-end. This approach has several advantages over working with a single database file:

- The developer can release updated versions of the user interface while users are still accessing the data. The only files that change during an upgrade are the front-end files. The back-end file remains untouched.

- Individual users can be given front-end files that are customized to their specific needs. For example, you can create separate front-end files for management and for the staff who conduct day to day data entry and edits. Additionally, users can create custom queries, forms, and reports yet still access a common back-end file.

- Network traffic is greatly reduced because the user interface elements are installed locally on each user's computer. The only network traffic are the requests for data from the tables in the back-end file. For multiuser environments this is a strong reason to use split databases as part of your distribution scheme.

## How to Split a Database

Before beginning, make a back-up copy of the original database and store it in a safe location. The target for the back-end file *must* be a shared folder that all computers in the group can access. It is best to start this process by moving a copy of the original Access database to one of the computers that will house the front-end file.

Step 1.       Open the original database file in Access.

Step 2.       From the **Database Tools** tab, in the **Move Data** group, choose **Access Database**.

Step 3.       Start the Database Splitter Wizard by choosing **Split Database** from the first dialog box.

Step 4.       In the **Create Back-End Database** dialog box, navigate to the target shared folder, then type a name for the *back-end* portion of the database (or accept the provided default). Choose **Split.**

 When naming the back-end file, Access will use the database file name and append it with *_be.accdb*. The original database file becomes the front-end.

Step 5.       Distribute copies of the front-end file to your users.

 If you relocate the back-end file after splitting the database, or if one or more of the work group computers uses a different network path to get to the back-end, you must use the **Linked Table Manager** to reestablish the links between front- and back-end files.

## How to Use the Linked Table Manager

This facility is used if the connection between front and back-end files is broken. This can happen if you rename the back-end file, move the back-end file, or work with a front-end database that uses a different URL to reference the back-end file location. The **Linked Table Manager** also supports creation of front-end databases that link to two or more back-end files. If the names of tables change on the back-end you cannot use the **Linked Table Manager**. You must delete the reference to the old tables in each front-end file and manually import the tables as linked references.

Step 1.     Open the front-end file that requires relinking to the back-end.

Step 2.     Right-click on any linked table and choose **Linked Table Manager** from the shortcut menu. The **Linked Table Manager** will appear similar to the following:

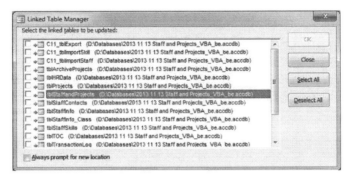

Step 3.     To relink specific tables, select them from the list of tables. To relink all tables, choose **Select All**.

Step 4.     If you need to simply relink tables without specifying a network location or back-end file name (this is rare), choose OK (this would complete the procedure). Otherwise check **Always prompt for new location**, then choose **OK**.

Step 5.     Navigate to the desired back-end file and choose **Open**. The **Linked Table Manager** will relink the selected table or tables.

## Annealing a Split Database

Under some circumstances you may find it necessary to recombine a split database—front and back-end files—into a single Access database file. This is done by removing the references to the linked tables in one of the front-end files and then importing the original tables back into that file.

Step 1.     Open one of the copies of the front-end file and move to the **Tables** area in the **Navigation Pane**.

Step 2.     Delete the reference to each table that is linked to the back-end file. Note that if your split database scheme involves linked tables from several back-end files you will need to keep track of the location of each table reference you delete.

Step 3.     Move to the **External Data** tab and from the **Import & Link** group, choose **Access.**

Step 4.     From the **Get External Data** dialog box, navigate to and select the file that constitutes the back-end of the original split database. Ensure that the **Import Tables, queries...** option is selected and choose **OK**.

Step 5.     On the **Import Objects** dialog box, in the **Tables** tab, select the table or tables to import. Alternatively use the **Select All** button to select all tables.

Step 6.     Choose **OK**.

# Glossary

**ACE (Access database Engine)**  This is the current database technology that underlies Access. It replaces the JET (Joint Enhancement Technology) engine from prior versions of Access. These engines mediate table structure, data storage, and queries.

**ADO (ActiveX Data Object)**  One of several data access objects (the other common one being DAO). ADO is a lightweight, object-oriented technology that provides access to other ODBC compliant databases such as Microsoft SQL Server and MySQL.

**Application**  The combination of a program *and* its data. When you combine tables and their data with user interface elements in an Access database you are creating an application.

**Argument**  A parameter which is passed to a sub or function procedure, or to a method of an object with the purpose of controlling some aspect of the procedure or method's actions.

**Argument List**  For sub or function procedures, or object methods that require one or more arguments, this is the formal list of arguments, arranged in the order in which they are expected when a call to the procedure or object method is made.

**Bound Object**  A form, report, or a control on such object that is connected to a data source. Forms and reports are bound to tables or queries while their controls are generally bound to one of the fields from that data source.

**Break Time (or Break Mode)**  During program execution, this is a time when the program flow has been interrupted. This may happen when a *breakpoint* is encountered, when the user presses **Ctrl Break**, or when an *untrapped error* occurs.

**Breakpoint**  A point set on an executable line of code within the VBA editor that halts program flow. Breakpoints are temporary and are lost when the current database file is closed.

**ByRef**  By Reference - when a variable is passed as an *argument* in an *argument list* in a manner that effectively passes the address of the variable. The effect is that the procedure may alter the value of the original variable.

**ByVal**  By Value - when a variable is passed as an *argument* in an *argument list* in a manner that effectively passes the value of the variable within a copy of the variable. The effect is that the copy may be altered within a procedure but the original value is unaltered.

**Call Stack**  A structure that tracks program execution when program flow moves between two or more sub or function procedures. This is necessary in order for program flow to correctly return to any jump point between procedures.

**Certificate**  A digital file that serves to establish trusted credentials for a developer or a company.

**Child**  In an object-oriented environment this is an object that is contained or owned by another object - typically called its *parent*.

| | |
|---|---|
| **Class** | In object oriented programming this is a template for defining a type. Classes are frequently used to define objects, so a form is an object of the **Form** class, the latter being a template in code that specifies the properties, methods, and events that make up all forms. |
| **Class Module** | A code module used to establish a class. Class modules are grouped with other *Modules* in the **Navigation Pane**. Technically, since an existing form or report can be *instantiated*, the code modules for these objects are also considered to be class modules. |
| **Coercion** | The process of forcing data into a particular data type. |
| **Collection** | In object oriented programming, this is a property of an object that manages one or more objects of the same type (for example a collection of controls on a form). Collections are typically given the plural form of the object name. Thus a form maintains a **Controls** collection that represents all of the control objects on the form. |
| **COM** | Component Object Model - a programming paradigm in Microsoft Windows that enable *Applications* to communicate programmatically, usually after being *instantiated* as an *object*. |
| **Compile** | The conversion of code into a machine-level or lower-level form for execution. The VBA editor complies all code before it is run. You can optionally force code to compile, which is a useful technique for discovering *Compile-Time Errors*. |
| **Compile-Time Error** | An error, usually in syntax, that may not be noticed by the VBA editor during code creation. Examples are un-terminated IF or Do structures, or undeclared variables when using *Explicit Variable Declaration*. |
| **Concatenation** | The process of combining the values of two or more variables or field values that physically combines them rather than performing an addition operation. For example, the concatenation of the values 123 and 456 result in 123456 while the addition of those values results in 579. |
| **Constant** | A named memory location of a particular data type that is declared and populated with a value once during program execution. Constants are different from *Variables* in that the latter may undergo unlimited changes to their values during program execution. |
| **Container** | In the context of object oriented programming, an object that contains other objects. Forms and reports are both *Containers* in that they contain controls. |
| **Cursor** | A database concept that refers to a structure that points to the current record in a table, query, or a record set. In client-server environments the cursor can usually be set to reside either on the server or client side. |
| **DAO (Data Access Object)** | One of several data access objects (the other common one being ADO). DAO is a native extension of the Microsoft Access ACE engine and can manage the table and query structure, as well as the data contained with tables and queries. Like ADO, DAO also supports connections to ODBC-compliant databases but ADO is a technology that requires less memory and executes faster. |

| | |
|---|---|
| **Data Source Name (DNS)** | A component of the Windows operating system that is a structure which contains information necessary to connect to a data source, such as a database server. DNS objects typically require drivers and are managed by the ODBC manager in the Windows Control Panel. |
| **Data Type** | A property of a *Variable* that specifies the type of data to be stored. In a highly-typed language such as VBA there are numerous data types, each optimized to store a particular type of data. Thus, some languages see the value "04 July 1776" as *String* (or character) data while VBA understands the value to be of the **Date** data type. |
| **Decision Structure** | In programming, a set of related *Keywords* that can control *Program Flow* based on the state of certain *Variables* or *Objects*. |
| **Delimiter** | A special symbol used to denote characters as representing values of a particular *Data Type*. In VBA, string data are delimited using double quotes while date/time data are delimited using the pound sign (#). Numeric data are not delimited. String data must be delimited otherwise the VBA editor interprets it as being the name of a variable or procedure. |
| **Design Time** | That time within the VBA editor when code is being created or edited. Code only runs during this time if you elicit it using the **Immediate Window**. |
| **Event** | A process that notifies an object of some action. Events are realized through an *Event Handler* which is a procedure associated with the object recognizing the event. |
| **Event Handler** | A procedure that is called when the parent object recognizes that a particular event has occurred. For example, the *Click* event for a command button is contained within a event handler named *Click*. Any code within this procedure runs if the command button is clicked by a user. |
| **Explicit Variable Declaration** | A configuration within a code module that requires the programmer to formally declare every variable. This approach can save the programmer much time in troubleshooting code as *Implicit Variable Declaration* creates variables as they are written in code. Spelling mistakes and typographical errors tend to create new variables when *Implicit Variable Declaration* is in effect. |
| **Fixed-length String** | A variable of the string *Data Type* that has a prefixed length. Such a variable may store string data up to but not exceeding this length. |
| **Function Procedure** | A unit of code that typically returns some value. Functions may have an *Argument List* and always return data of a particular *Data Type*. Functions may be built-in and part of the application or created by the user or programmer. |
| **General Declarations** | A section of a *General* or *Class Module* used to declare *Variables, Constants* or *Objects* that will have public *Scope*. No executable code may be placed in this section of a module. |
| **General Module** | A module which is not associated with a form, report, or a class. General Modules contain VBA code (sub and/or function procedures) which have global *Scope*. |

| | |
|---|---|
| **Implicit Variable Declaration** | The default method of creating variables in VBA. Variables may be created without the DIM statement and without assigning a *Data Type*. Variables created this way are assigned the *Variant* data type. Using Implicit Variable Declaration is considered sloppy programming and the *Explicit Variable Declaration* is strongly recommended. |
| **Instantiate** | The act of creating an instance of an object. For example you can create a variable of the Form *Data Type* and then instantiate this object by referring to an existing, open form. Once instantiated, the object may be manipulated and such manipulations affect the real form object. |
| **Interface** | In object-oriented program, this is the set of input and output properties and methods offered by an object that control how the object interacts with your code. |
| **Intrinsic Constant** | A *Constant* that is built-in, either to Access, VBA, or some other object or application. In VBA, intrinsic constants begin with the prefix *vb* (Example: vbYesNoCancel). Intrinsic constants make reading VBA code easier as they replace values (typically numeric) with human-readable names. In the example above, vbYesNoCancel is an intrinsic constant of the **MsgBox** function and specifies the **Buttons** argument. The actual value of vbYesNoCancel is *3*. |
| **JET** | Joint Enhancement Technology was the original data engine in Microsoft Access. Since Access 2007 it has been replaced by the *ACE* engine. |
| **Keyword** | A *Reserved Word* in a programming language that refers to a built-in component of the programming language. |
| **Library** | A file (typically of the DLL extension) that contains the *Class* information required to *Instantiate* an *Object*. In Microsoft Windows, all *COM* objects have one or more libraries associated with them. |
| **Lifetime** | The time during program flow in which a variable or an object is accessible and can store data. Lifetime is usually limited to the time in which a procedure containing the declarative statements that create the variable or object runs, although it is possible to elevate the lifetime of such objects to longer time periods. Lifetime is conceptually related to *Scope*. |
| **Literal** | Generally applied when referring to an *Argument* in an *Argument List*, a literal is an actual value as opposed to a variable storing a value. Example, the *Argument* "Washington" is a string literal while the argument strCapitalCity refers to a variable which may contain the value "Washington". |
| **Logic Error** | An error that is due to a flaw that results in the code running incorrectly but not leaving *Run Time*. Such errors are generally a result of flawed thinking on the part of the programmer. |
| **Member** | A member of an *Object* refers to a *Property, Method*, or an *Event* of that object. A object's *Members* refers to the total collection of properties, methods, and events of that object class. |
| **Method** | An action that can be performed by an object. Methods usually take verbs as their names. For example, the **Open** method of a Form object forces a form to open. |

| | |
|---|---|
| **Modal** | In operating systems, a modal object forces the user to interact with it. Message Boxes are typically modal - the user must click on the message box before interacting with any other element within the current *Application*. |
| **Module** | A collection of *Procedures* and a *General Declaration* section that constitute a unit of code. In VBA, each form and report contains a *Module*. You may also create *General* and *Class Modules*. |
| **Object** | A combination of code and data that expresses some functionality. In Microsoft Windows, nearly every item a user interacts with is an object. Objects are the fundamental unit of *Object Oriented Programming*. |
| **OOP (Object Oriented Programming)** | A programming approach that utilizes *Objects*. OOP is the dominant programming approach across all operating systems and languages. |
| **Parent** | An *Object* that *Contains* other objects. Typically used when discussing a Form or a Report and its relationship to subforms, subreports, and controls. |
| **Procedure** | A body of programming code that performs a specific task or function. There are two types: Sub and Function procedures. The former performs a task without returning a specific value while the latter always returns a value. |
| **Program Flow** | The stepwise execution of a program. Programs typically have one or more starting points and may also have one or more end points (which depend upon the actions of *Decision Structures*. Program flow may be interrupted by *Breakpoints* or errors. Flow may also move between *Procedures*. Program Flow occurs only during *Run Time*. |
| **Project** | In VBA a project refers to the *Application* plus its VBA code. An Access database file maps to a VBA project, as does an Excel workbook. |
| **Property** | An attribute of an object. Properties relate to how an object appears or behaves, for example the ForeColor property of a text box object sets font color. Most properties are read/write meaning you can test the property value or change it. There are read-only properties however. |
| **Reserved Word** | In a programming language, these are the keywords and user-defined terms that have meaning to the code interpreter. For example, when a programmer establishes *Variables* and creates sub and/or function *Procedures*, their names become reserved words. |
| **Run Time** | The time when a program is executing. This is opposed to *Design Time* or *Break Time* when *Program Flow* ceases. |
| **Run Time Error** | An error condition that arises when the code is executing. Run time errors cannot be caught during *Design Time* or when code is *Compiled*. They differ from *Logic Errors* in that they can be *Trapped*. |
| **Scope** | The visibility of an element such as a *Variable, Constant, Procedure* or *Object* during *Run Time*. Scope refers to whether another portion of code, typically in another *Procedure* or *Module* can reference the other element. Scope is closely related to *Lifetime* and like lifetime can be elevated to increase the visibility of the element. |
| **Statement** | A distinct unit of programming code. Statements generally occupy a separate line in code and are the fundamental unit of organization for *Procedures*. |

| | |
|---|---|
| **Sub Procedure** | A type of *Procedure* that elicits some action but once completed does not return a value to the code that called or evoked it. |
| **Transaction** | In database applications, a transaction is a unit of table activity that is treated as a whole. Transactions are processed by the database in an all or none manner. Transactions effectively wrap INSERT, UPDATE, DELETE, or APPEND operations into a logical block. If an error occurs while processing a transaction that updates 10,000 records, none of the updates are processed. |
| **Trapped Error** | An error that can be managed using an error handler. Almost all *Run Time Errors* are trappable. |
| **Unit Testing** | An approach to writing code that focuses on creating smaller, functional units of code (*Procedures*) which are fully tested as they are created. |
| **Untrapped Error** | An error that is not processed by an error handler and causes *Program Flow* to enter *Break Mode*. Some errors cannot be trapped as in the example of a user unplugging their computer from the power supply while your code is running. |
| **Variable** | A data storage element that is identified by a name and a *Data Type*. Variables are similar to *Constants* except their stored value may change during program execution. |
| **Variable-length String** | A variable of the string *Data Type* that lacks a prefixed length. Such a variable may store string data up to but not exceeding a size that is generally defined by the programming language. For example, string variables can store up to 2 billion characters. |
| **Variant** | A *Data Type* that is flexible and may store many types of data. Variants may require more memory than a typed *Variable*. |
| **Zero-length String** | A *Variable* of the string data type that contains no value, or the value is equal to the empty double quotes, "". |

# Appendix A | Staff and Projects Database

The samples in this manual illustrate a simple staff and projects database – a design that might commonly be used in an organization that tracks information about staff (contact methods and skills) as well as information about projects (here the main interest is in the staffing of projects as well as the budget for a project). A copy of this database may be downloaded from www.sycamoretechnicalpress.com

The basic relationships between the tables used in the sample database appear in the following illustration.

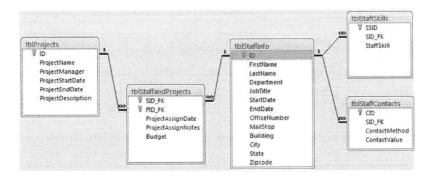

The structure of the 5 tables, and if applicable, the indices used to maintain uniqueness among rows, are presented below.

## tblStaffInfo

This table, along with tblProjects, can be considered the two main tables in the staff and projects database. A primary key affords an easy way to relate a staff record to other tables and an index based on staff first and last name as well as department enforce uniqueness for each row.

| Field Name | Data Type | Description |
| --- | --- | --- |
| ID | AutoNumber | Primary Key |
| FirstName | Text | |
| LastName | Text | |
| Department | Text | |
| JobTitle | Text | |
| StartDate | Date/Time | |
| EndDate | Date/Time | |
| OfficeNumber | Text | |
| MailStop | Text | |
| Building | Text | |
| City | Text | |

There are two indices for tblStaffInfo. The primary key is automatically created by Access. The index **Staff** asserts that no two records may contain the same staff first and last name and department.

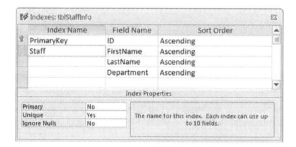

| Index Name | Field Name | Sort Order |
| --- | --- | --- |
| PrimaryKey | ID | Ascending |
| Staff | FirstName | Ascending |
| | LastName | Ascending |
| | Department | Ascending |

Index Properties

| | |
| --- | --- |
| Primary | No |
| Unique | Yes |
| Ignore Nulls | No |

The name for this index. Each index can use up to 10 fields.

## tblProjects

Along with tblStaffInfo this table constitutes the other major table in the Staff and Projects database. Both tables store information about the two realms the database focuses on. Like the tblStaffInfo table, a second index **Project** enforces uniqueness by assuming the combination of project name, project manager, and start date will not be repeated.

| Field Name | Data Type | Description |
| --- | --- | --- |
| ID | AutoNumber | Primary Key |
| ProjectName | Text | |
| ProjectManager | Text | |
| ProjectStartDate | Date/Time | |
| ProjectEndDate | Date/Time | |
| ProjectDescription | Text | |

The indexes for tblProjects appears as:

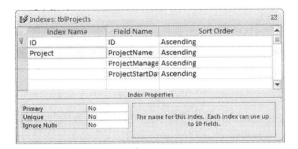

## tblStaffContact

This table relates the one-to-many ways you can contact each staff member. An index based on the foreign key for the staff ID, the contact method, and the contact value, ensure that no two rows are duplicated.

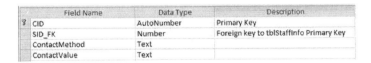

The index appears as follows:

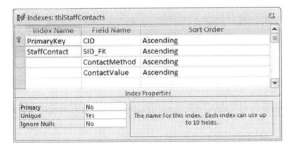

## tblStaffSkills

Similar to tblStaffContacts, this table stores any skills associated with each staff member.

The index, based on the staff foreign key and staff skill, ensures uniqueness for each row:

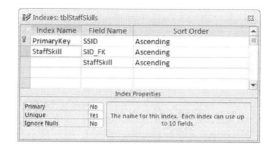

## tblStaffandProjects

The final table is the only bridge table in this design. Its purpose is to manage the information that relates to project staffing. Each project may have one or more staff assigned to it, and ultimately, each staff member may be assigned to zero or more projects. It is also the only table in the database design to utilize two fields which together make up the table's primary key: the foreign key to the tblStaffInfo primary key and the foreign key to the tblProjects primary key. Using these two fields together ensures uniqueness among the rows and enforces the logical requirement that no staff can be assigned to a project more than once. This simple design removes any requirement for an additional index to enforce uniqueness among the records.

Further, in this design the budget field implies that each staff member is given an individual budget for their part in a project. Recall from the discussion on banded reports that even given this configuration, with a project staffed by several members from the same department, one can easily generate a report that groups project staffing information by department, with the purpose of providing totals of the budget amount both by staff, by department, and by project.

# Appendix B | ODBC Data Sources

Connecting to an Open Database Connectivity (or ODBC) compliant database server is generally mediated through a DSN (Data Source Name). DSN's are managed in Windows using the **ODBC Data Source Administrator** (or in Windows 8 it is referred to by the title **ODBC Data Sources**). This is a component of the Windows operating system and is located in the **Control Panel**. In 64-bit operating systems both a 64-bit and a 32-bit version are shipped, although the 32-bit version is access via the command line.

 If you are creating a DSN on a 64-bit system you may need to work with the 32-bit version as some ODBC database vendors only release 32-bit versions, or newer 64-bit versions may not work properly with 32-bit versions of Microsoft Access running on a 64-bit platform.

All major databases comply to the ODBC standard and each requires a driver in order to mediate the connection. A DSN is a file, either made available on a computer-by-computer or user-by-user basis that references the appropriate driver and stores information required to mediate the connection. Once a DNS has been established and tested, you can refer to it in VBA code (there are several examples of this in Chapter 11). One strong utility to this approach is that any sensitive user and password information required to make the ODBC connection is stored in the DSN and in the case of the password, is not readable. This is in contrast to specifying the ODBC parameters with a **ConnectionString** property or an **Open** method in ADO or DAO (respectively) where unless your code is password protected, these arguments can be viewed by end users.

## Precursors to Creating a DNS

Creating a DNS first requires that the appropriate driver has been installed on the local computer. Once the driver has been installed, you use the **ODBC Data Source Administrator** or the **ODBC Data Sources** facility in Windows 8 to create the DNS. Drivers are generally installed by downloading the appropriate install file from the database vendor. For example, to install a 32-bit MySQL driver you first visit the MySQL.com website and locate the downloadable Windows Installer for the 32-bit ODBC driver.

Another obvious prerequisite is that you must have the appropriate permissions granted on the server you are intending to connect to. Unless you are also the administrator of that server, you will need to seek permission to connect to the target database. Ensure that the appropriate rights are granted as well. For example, if you must update records the administrator should grant you UPDATE permission.

## Determining 32-bit or 64-bit Status

To determine whether your operating system is 32-bit or 64-bit:

Step 1.        From the **Start** menu, select **Computer**.

Step 2.        On the **Computer** dialog, choose **System Properties**.

The type of operating system installed will appear in the **System** area under the heading **System Type**.

To determine the version of Microsoft Access you are using:

Step 1.        From Access, select the **File** menu.

Step 2.        Select **Help**.

The type of Access installed will appear under the heading **About Microsoft Access**.

## Running the ODBC Administrator

You need to know whether your operating system is 32-bit or 64-bit before proceeding. If you are using a 32-bit operating system you must work with 32-bit OBDC drivers.

| If using | Follow this procedure |
| --- | --- |
| **Windows 7/32-bit using 32-bit drivers** **Windows 7/64-bit using 64-bit drivers** | Open the **ODBC Data Source Administrator** (on 64-bit Windows 7, this is available from the **Control Panel**). |
| **Windows 7/64-bit using 32-bit drivers** | Go to the command prompt and enter the command: c:\windows\sysWOW64\odbcad32.exe. |
| **Windows 8** | Open the **ODBC Data Source Sources** from the **Control Panel** and choose either the 32-bit or the 64-bit OBDC Data Source Administrator. |

## How to Create a DSN

As mentioned, you should determine whether you need to work with a 32-bit or a 64-bit driver before proceeding. If either your operating system or your version of Access are 32-bit, you should install and work with a 32-bit driver. For purposes of illustration, this procedure will assume working with 32-bit drivers on a 64-bit version of Windows 7.

Step 1.    Open the appropriate ODBC administrator using the previous table as a guide. The **OBDC Data Source Administrator** will appear similar to the following:

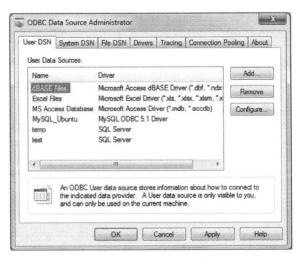

| Tab | Description |
|---|---|
| **User DNS** | Manages DSN connections associated with a single user on the current computer. |
| **System DSN** | Manages DNS connections for the computer - available to all users. |
| **File DSN** | Creates and manages DNS *files* which can be distributed to other users on other computers provided all have access to the same ODBC driver. |
| **Drivers** | Lists all currently-installed ODBC drivers. |
| **Tracing** | Manages connection tracing which is useful for debugging a troublesome ODBC connection. If an application that uses ODCB is open before tracing is enabled, that application is not tracked. |
| **Connection Pooling** | An advanced feature that can increase performance by allowing applications to access a driver that has been *pooled*. This eliminates the time spent opening and closing an ODBC connection. |
| **About** | Lists the version and DLL file source for the components of Windows that manage ODBC. |

Step 2.    If desired, ensure that the appropriate driver is installed by locating it from the list of installed drivers on the **Drivers** tab.

Creating a DSN is essentially the same for the three options, except when you create a **File DSN** you specify a file name and location as part of the process. The steps that follow will assume you are creating a **User DSN**.

Step 3.     Move to the **User DSN** tab and choose **Add**.

Step 4.     In the **Create New Data Source** dialog, choose the appropriate driver, then choose **Finish**.

The next steps depend upon the driver you selected. Steps 5 through 7 will assume connection to a MySQL database server. To illustrate how individual drivers are different, Steps 8 through 12 will pick up from this point but illustrate connection to a Microsoft SQL Server.

**Establishing a User DNS for a MySQL Database:**

Once the MySQL driver has been selected, the **MySQL Connector/ODBC Data Source Configuration** dialog box will appear similar to the following:

Step 5.     Complete the text fields using the following table as a guide:

| Field | Description |
|---|---|
| Data Source Name | A descriptive term that will identify this DSN connection. This is the name used in VBA to refer to a specific DSN. |
| Description | Optional text description for this DSN. |
| TCP/IP Server | Use if connecting to a server via regular network protocol. On some topologies you can refer to the server by name, otherwise enter the IP address of the server and the port number (if not using the default). |
| Named Pipe | The alternative method of connecting to the server. Use only if a named pipe has been established for this connection. |
| User | The username required to access the ODBC database. |
| Password | The password associated with the user account for the ODBC database. |
| Database | The database on the server you will connect to. DNS connections are always database specific. |
| Test | Used to verify that the connection and parameters for the DSN are correct. |
| Details | Expands a set of advanced options. |

Step 6.     Complete the required fields and use the **Test** button to ensure that the parameters are correct and that you can connect to the ODBC database. Choose **OK** when done.

Step 7.     The new **File DSN** will appear in the list of DNS's on the **File DSN** tab.

**Establishing a User DNS for a Microsoft SQL Server Database:**

Once the SQL Server driver has been selected, the **Create a New Data Source to SQL Server** dialog box will appear similar to the following:

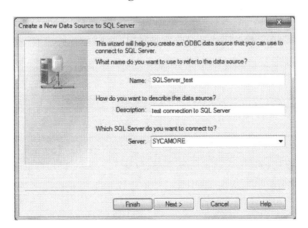

Step 8.     Complete the **Name**, **Description**, and **Server** fields - these have the same purpose as for the MySQL example with the exception that any named server will appear in the drop down box. If necessary, manually complete the **Server** field by entering a valid server name or IP address. Choose **Next**. The second dialog box for this process will appear similar to the following:

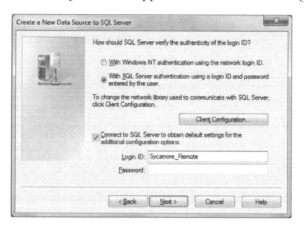

Step 9.     SQL Server may accept one or more authentication schemes (based on Window NT/network login or SQL Server account-specific). Choose the appropriate scheme and if required, complete the **Login ID** and **Password** sections. Choose **Next** when ready.

Step 10.    In the third dialog, select a database to connect to. You will only see those databases for which permissions have been granted. Choose **Next** when done.

Step 11.    The fourth dialog in this process involves server settings such as the language, log file location, and encryption method. Adjust these settings if necessary then select **Finish**. The final dialog box in this process will appear similar to the following:

Step 12. Test the data source connection. If problems arise step back through the process and correct any problems. Otherwise choosing **OK** will complete the process. The new **User DSN** will appear in the list of DSN's on the **User DNS** tab.

## Modifying a DSN

Any User, System, or File DSN that you create can be modified.

Step 1. Open the appropriate **ODBC Data Source** application as discussed on page 241.

Step 2. Move to the appropriate tab (either **User DSN**, **System DSN**, or **File DSN**) and select the DSN to modify.

Step 3. Choose **Configure**.

Depending upon the driver, the configure process will step you back through the dialog or dialog boxes used to initially create the DSN, with the exception that the fields will be completed in the initial information. Change what entries require editing and complete the setup process.

## Removing a DSN

Any User, System, or File DSN that you create can be deleted.

| Step 1. | Open the appropriate **ODBC Data Source** application as discussed on page 241. |
| Step 2. | Move to the appropriate tab (either **User DSN**, **System DSN**, or **File DSN**) and select the DSN to delete. |
| Step 3. | Choose **Remove**. When prompted choose **Yes** to delete or **No** to cancel the operation. |

# Index

# About the Author

F. Mark Schiavone was originally trained as a research scientist, and in that capacity he began constructing database applications and analyzing complex data sets over 30 years ago. His database skills include Microsoft Access, Microsoft SQL Server and MySQL and he has constructed applications using those platforms for clients in large to mid-size organizations, including the US Department of Education, the National Weather Service, and the International Monetary Fund. He has authored over 30 training titles in topics such as Microsoft Access, Microsoft Word, Microsoft Excel, and in the VBA programming language. Each title was designed with the busy office technology worker in mind and focuses on important and useful tasks.

Along with his partner John he has restored three stone houses (two of which were 18th century while the most recent house dates from 1835), reroofed a loafing barn, disassembled and reassembled a corn crib, and built several frame houses, additions or outbuildings. He has designed every new structure built on their property. He is a passionate all weather, high mileage motorcyclist and is usually the only motorcyclist on the local roads when the temperature is below 25° F.

Cover design by Martha A. Loomis.

Made in the USA
Middletown, DE
27 March 2017